THE SPIRITUAL EXERCISES OF
St. Ignatius

TRANSLATED BY

ANTHONY MOTTOLA, PH.D.

INTRODUCTION BY

ROBERT W. GLEASON, S.J.

IMAGE BOOKS
DOUBLEDAY
NEW YORK   LONDON   TORONTO   SYDNEY   AUCKLAND

AN IMAGE BOOK
PUBLISHED BY DOUBLEDAY
a division of Bantam Doubleday Dell Publishing Group, Inc.
1540 Broadway, New York, New York 10036

IMAGE, DOUBLEDAY, and the portrayal of a deer drinking
from a stream are trademarks of Doubleday, a division of
Bantam Doubleday Dell Publishing Group, Inc.

First Image edition published February 1964.
This Image edition published November 1989.

Imprimi Potest:	John J. McGinty, S.J.
	Praep. Prov. Neo Eboracenis
	May 15, 1963
Nihil obstat:	John P. Sullivan, M.A.
	Censor Deputatus
Imprimatur:	✠Francis Cardinal Spellman
	Archibishop of New York
	October 16, 1963

ISBN 0-385-02436-3
Library of Congress Catalog Card Number 64-12784

"... the mind and heart of Ignatian spirituality is *distinguished* service of Christ."

—*Robert W. Gleason, S.J.*

In his incisive Introduction to this classic work of Christian spirituality, Fr. Robert W. Gleason states that: "The Spiritual Exercises touch on so many important aspects of the spiritual life that they may justly be called a summary of the most profound principles of ascetical theology . . . The central positive principle is the imitation of Christ our Lord, the exemplary cause of all Christian perfection."

A complete guide and framework for achieving Christian perfection, the *Exercises* are divided into four weeks of meditations which are generally directed by a retreat master. The first week is designed to help the retreatant to purify his soul and put his life in order; the aim of the second week is to lead the soul to a greater knowledge of and love for Jesus Christ; the third week is devoted to freeing the will from the psychological obstacles which stand in the way of a generous decision to follow Christ; and the fourth week is intended to purify the heart in the highest degree from false attachment to creatures, goods, or worldly ambition and honor.

The four key meditations of the *Exercises*—without which a retreat would not be Ignatian—are contemplations on the Kingdom of God, the Two Standards (of Christ and of Satan), the Three Classes of Men, and The Three Modes of Humility. Crowning the whole work of the *Exercises* is the Contemplation to Obtain Love, which synthesizes the total effort of the four weeks so that the retreatant resolves to live a life exclusively for God in joyous service.

The first step in the essential method of the Ignatian approach to spirituality is a whole-hearted desire for distinguished and generous service of Christ, and this desire is perfected and developed through *active* participation in the meditations given, the maintenance of complete silence, the constant observance of the movements of the soul from indifference through compunction to devotion to Christ, contemplation of His life and reform of one's own life and, finally, the union of the will in perfect familiarity with God.

The high praise that has been lavished on the *Exercises* through the years by religious and lay people is a continuing tribute to the worth of these meditations as a precise tool for re-energizing the spiritual life. This new translation provides a clear, orderly, and modern version of the timeless classic.

THE SPIRITUAL EXERCISES OF
St. Ignatius

CONTENTS

FIRST WEEK

SECOND WEEK

THIRD WEEK

FOURTH WEEK

RULES

APPENDIX

INTRODUCTION TO THE SPIRITUAL EXERCISES

The history of the composition of the Spiritual Exercises is, in a certain sense, the history of a soul's journey from spiritual childhood to spiritual adulthood. Probably almost every Christian knows the story of the conversion of St. Ignatius from a relatively worldly life to one of serious spiritual effort.

However, the providential preparation of Ignatius as an instrument in the counterreformation of the Church and as a spiritual leader began long before his well-known conversion. His whole life was oriented to this end and the various influences of racial and family background, training and experience helped to mold the future author of the *Spiritual Exercises*. In 1491 Ignatius was born at the family castle of Loyola in the Basque country. The family belonged to provincial nobility whose members had fought with the kings of Castile since 1200. Hugo Rahner notes that Ignatius kept, all his life, an aristocratic sense of form, order, and loyalty along with a practical, realistic grasp of problems, people, and principles which reflect both the nobility of his background and the fact that it was *provincial* nobility, close to the realities of life.[1] The traditions of soldiering characteristic of his family, members of which had fought in Hungary and in Naples, are also evidenced in Ignatius' strong sense of duty, of obedience, and of high-minded chivalry. Although Ignatius' father

[1] Hugo Rahner, *The Spirituality of St. Ignatius Loyola*, Newman, Westminster, 1953, pp. 1–16. This book, together with *A Key to the Study of the Spiritual Exercises* by Ignacio Iparraguirre, will prove most helpful to one desirous of making a further study of the Exercises. A helpful commentary on the Exercises in English is A. Ambruzzi's *A Companion to the Spiritual Exercises of St. Ignatius*, Mangalore, 1928.

had envisioned for him, the youngest son, the career of a cleric, as was frequently the case for the cadets of noble families, the youthful Ignatius far preferred the attractions of military exploits. His temperament seems to have been merry and carefree, and his service as a page, which he began at sixteen years of age in 1507 at the court of a relative, Don Juan Velasquez who was attached to the royal court, perhaps accentuated these attitudes. He seems to have fallen in love there with a lady of royal blood, perhaps *Doña* Caterina, daughter of Philip the Fair. At the court, although he remained loyal to his faith, he seems, by his own confession, to have enjoyed gambling, dueling, fulfilling the exacting court ritual, and romances with women rather than the clerical occupations his father had hoped he would embrace. The period of court no doubt enhanced his chivalrous attitude and the longing he felt to excel in some line, even if only in the service of an earthly king.

After his return to the family castle at Loyola, Ignatius' attitude seems to have remained rather worldly; he was torn between his sense of honor and the inclinations of the flesh. What his failings were at this period we cannot ascertain with certitude since Ignatius does not specify them. However, while very little of his time was devoted to spiritual things, he did struggle to preserve that magnanimous greatness of soul and longing for nobility and distinction always characteristic of him. He was always free from attachment to money or anything base. In 1517 Ignatius took service in the army and in May of 1521 he received a leg wound in the border skirmish of Pampeluna, defending that citadel against the French. Ignatius came back to Loyola to recuperate and it was here that his real conversion began, a conversion providentially prepared from the beginning in his natural gifts and the various experiences of his life.

Instead of novels, which the castle library could not furnish, Ignatius was given the *Life of Christ* and a collection of the lives of the saints. As a result of reading these books in the castle of Loyola, Ignatius began to form the main lines of his Spiritual Exercises, especially his doctrine of the election of a state of life. The conflict of spirits which he suffered here, drawn as he was on the one hand to the worldly joys he had previously known, and on the other by the forceful spirit of God, moved Ignatius to reconsider the values he had previously accepted as normal. Having decided on the permanent reform of his rather worldly life, he set about the task with characteristic energy.

He resolved to make a pilgrimage to Jerusalem and as a first step on the journey set out for Monserrat, a famous sanctuary to our Lady in Catalonia. Then he disposed of his worldly goods, clothed himself in a pilgrim's sackcloth garment, and made a general confession, and his "knight's vigil of love" before Mary's altar. He then took ship for Barcelona and on the way stopped off at a small town called Manresa. Delayed from proceeding to Rome by the new Pope, Adrian VI, and prevented from entering Barcelona by an outbreak of the plague there, he decided to remain a few days in Manresa. These few days stretched into ten months with results that are still reverberating around the world.

From March of 1522 to February of 1523 he remained at Manresa, praying and doing penance. Whatever he found useful for his own spiritual life, he wrote down in the hope that it might also be useful to others. In the course of this year of silence Ignatius meditated much upon two central themes of his Spiritual Exercises: the Kingdom of God and the Two Standards, that of Christ and that of Satan, thereby preparing himself for combat with the spirit of the world.

During his stay at Manresa, Ignatius was favored with many extraordinary spiritual, even mystical, experiences. Profiting by them himself, he also gradually evolved a method of sharing with others his insights into the Christian life, for his book, the *Spiritual Exercises*, was to form the basis of most retreats given to priests, religious, and lay people. From this period we can date at least some of the Exercises: the concatenation of meditations on the mysteries of our Lord's life as seen in the Second Week and the key meditations of the Kingdom and the Two Standards. Some authorities, in fact, date the whole general architecture of the Exercises from this time, maintaining that Ignatius here settled upon the five major themes which structure them: Creation, Mankind, The Kingdom of God, Christ. The Trinity.

For an understanding of the Exercises it will help to have clearly in mind their general outline. They are divided into four "weeks" of meditations, but the term "week" is flexible; they may last more than a month; on the other hand, they are often reduced to eight days, as in the case of the annual retreat for religious men and women. The first week corresponds roughly to what is called the purgative way in the spiritual life; i.e., it is devoted to purifying the soul and putting one's life in order. In the second and third weeks the meditations are mostly drawn from the public life and Passion of Christ, and in the fourth week from His risen life. The Exercises open with a consideration of the principle and foundation on which all else is to rest, which is to put all else in perspective, namely: what is man's final end? how are all creatures related to this end, and what attitude of soul should a man have to enable him to use creatures effectively for that end? Having thus gone to the heart of the matter, man's absolute dependence on God. Ignatius proceeds to outline meditations for four weeks of the Exercises. The aim of the meditations of the first week is to arouse sorrow and contrition in the one making the Exercises as he reflects on the disorder of his life, his sins, and how he has failed to move effectively toward his final end. For this purpose Ignatius sets down for this week meditation on the sin of Adam and Eve, of the angels, on man's personal sins, death, hell, and so on. This week is designed to purify the soul, root out inordinate attachments to creatures, and enable one to amend his life through grateful love and surrender to Christ the Redeemer. With these dispositions of soul, one is prepared to undertake the second week of the Exercises or retreat.

The aim of the second week is to persuade the exercitant to an interior knowledge and love of the person of Jesus Christ, so that he may adapt his life to the model, identify himself with Christ as the concrete norm of Christian perfection. This assimilation to Christ is brought about by a series of meditations on His private and public life, and by the four key meditations on the Kingdom, the Two Standards, and Three Classes of Men, and the Three Modes of Humility. The Kingdom meditation is designed to arouse the greatest enthusiasm for close following of Christ in poverty and humility, conquering the obstacles to His Kingdom in one's own soul and preparing for the Apostolate. The meditation on the Two Standards examines Satan's ruses and Christ's plan for the world and is aimed at a decision which the exercitant is to make: the following of Christ in service to the Church, with discretion and a knowledge of the devices Satan uses to draw men away from Christ. The meditation on the Three Classes of Men is intended to free the will from the psychological obstacles and illusions which would prevent a generous decision to follow Christ intimately. The meditation on the Three Modes of Humility, or subjection to God, is intended to purify the heart in the highest degree and form an attachment to perfection that will lead the exercitant to choose only that which *best* leads to his final end, the possession of God. It is a description of what it means to follow the Cross.

The third week of the Exercises is concerned with the Passion of our Lord and is intended to confirm the exercitant in the options he has taken to follow Christ more closely by increasing his grateful love for Christ and his sorrow for his sins through study of Christ's sufferings.

The fourth week of the Exercises develops meditations on the Risen Life of Christ and is intended to engender unselfish love, joy in Christ's glory, and an unchanging trust in Christ the Consoler.

Crowning the whole work of the Exercises is the Contemplation to Obtain Love, which synthesizes the movement of the four weeks so that one lives one's life exclusively for God in joyous service, finding Him in all things and all things in Him. The cycle of the Exercises is now completed; the assimilation of the soul to God, it is hoped, is final, and the soul is fixed in a permanent state of divine consolation, given wholly over to His love and service.

Although the general structure of the Exercises may well have been completed by 1523, Ignatius was to know a long period of spiritual growth and enrichment before his book would be finished. He was to carry his notes with him on a journey to Jerusalem, and resume his schooling, studying philosophy at Alcala, and, from 1528 to 1533, philosophy and theology at Paris. By 1535 the book of the Exercises was complete. At Paris, probably, he developed the meditation on the Kingdom more fully, giving it its present form. It was here, too, that he added what we know as the foundation, that prelude to the Exercises on which Ignatius laid such great store, since it embodied the fundamental attitude which would govern a fruitful making of the Exercises. At Paris, the study of the Sacred Scriptures also doubtless aided in his shaping the meditations on the life of Christ and the Two Standards. Confronted at Paris with the principles of the Protestant Reformers, Ignatius added his "Rules for Thinking with the Church." In process of evolution from 1521 to 1535, the little book of the Exercises is the fruit of much thought, and even more spiritual experience.

A man of few ideas, but of immense practical genius, St. Ignatius turned his powers to the formation of apostolic and prayerful men. Throughout his life he was to use the Exercises to guide himself and others and it was always his intention that the Exercises be *given* by a retreat master who was familiar with them and could guide the retreatant, not simply *read* by the retreatant. At Paris he gave them to his first companions, the first fathers of the Society of Jesus, and this as well as other experiences in giving them, together with his personal mystical intuitions, contributed to the molding of their details. In the ultimate analysis the contribution which "the least Society" of Jesus has made to art and to civilization, to spirituality, and to thought, derives from these Exercises. In them St. Ignatius' personal insights into ascetical theology found their clearest expression; in them, too, each new generation of Jesuits is formed according to the spirit of St. Ignatius.

It was at one time the fashion to study in detail the sources supposedly used by the saint in the composition of the Exercises, some scholars even suggesting that there was very little of anything really original in the book. Whole sections of the Exercises were alleged to have been drawn from contemporary sources such as Cisneros, Erasmus, Alonzo de Madrid, and others. However Ignatius himself tells us clearly where he found his inspiration. In addition to the interior illumination of grace, the sifted experiences, his own and those of others to whom he had given the Exercises, Ignatius drew chiefly from three books: *The Imitation of Christ*, Ludolph of Saxony's *Life of Christ* and *The Golden Legend* of Jacopo de Voragine. Ignatius tells us that he first made the acquaintance of the *Imitation of Christ* during his stay at Manresa. There is no doubt that its influence on his thinking was profound, for he referred to it as the devotional book he liked most and echoes of its doctrines appear throughout the Exercises, especially in the tender love of Jesus inculcated in the second and third week.

The German Carthusian Ludolph of Saxony's *Life of Christ* had been translated into Spanish by Fray Ambrose Montesino in 1503 and we can easily trace its influence upon the thought of Ignatius. While convalescing in the family castle at Loyola from the leg wound received at Pampeluna he read the book with avidity, copying in red ink the words of the New Testament which so movingly brought Christ's deeds and words before him with their divinely inspired power; the words spoken by our Lady he copied in blue. He made copious excerpts from Ludolph's book, prayed over them at great length, and settled firmly in his soul the principles enunciated by them. His temperament had always been characterized by great-heartedness, generosity, "noblesse," even during his youth when he had led a somewhat sinful life. Now, under the influence of Christ's drawing power, this generosity, this aristocratic reverence for God's majesty, and this freedom of spirit were to be turned to divine pursuits.

Perhaps the most evident catalyst in this process was *The Golden Legend*, which Ignatius read in the Spanish translation of Goberto Vagad. Once he had learned of the great deeds that Augustine, Dominic, and Francis had done for Christ, his natural magnanimity of soul was elevated and inflamed. A new type of emulation was opened to him, worlds apart from the duels over ladies and the games of the court that had hitherto moved him to excel in "honor." His pil-

grimage journal notes that he could not efface from his mind
the question: could I not do what Francis did, could I not accomplish what Dominic did?

He was especially attracted by the extraordinary feats of
penance performed by the Egyptian monks of the desert,
whose lives and deeds were recounted in *The Golden Legend*. These monks, whose heroic renunciation appealed to
him so strongly, were seen by Ignatius as the most chivalrous
"Knights of the Cross" of Christ. Longing for more and more
difficult things to accomplish for Christ and to take the diffi-
culty of the enterprise as a gauge of his love, he planned to
make a pilgrimage to Jerusalem to see and touch the holy
places where the words of Christ had been uttered and the
Cross of Christ had been planted. Filled with desire "to do
great things in the service of God such as had been done by
St. Onuphrius"—one of his favorites among the saints whose
lives he had read in *The Golden Legend*, Ignatius described
himself at this period as possessing a heart inflamed with
love of God. The natural nobility was, under the influence of
grace, being transformed into a supernatural generosity.
Through his future writings, phrases like "the *greater* glory of
God," "what *more* can I do for Christ?" and "what conduces
more to the salvation of my soul?" will occur repeatedly. The
foundation for this preoccupation with extra-generous service,
with conspicuously large-hearted devotion of Christ, while
laid in Ignatius' nature, was undoubtedly stimulated by his
reading of *The Golden Legend*.

Two of the most important and characteristically Ignatian
meditations of the Exercises are the Kingdom of Christ and
the Two Standards. Both clearly reveal the influence of *The
Golden Legend*. The idea of warring under the banner of
Christ which we find in the Kingdom had fascinated Ignatius
even before Manresa. On the title page of *The Golden Legend*, Christ Crucified appears with the translator's description
of Him as the King of Kings. His Cross is there described as a
"royal standard," and He Himself appeals for a great-
hearted "conquest of the world." As Ignatius studied the
spiritual warriors described in this book he must have reflected often on that title page, echoes of which are heard so

clearly in his famous meditation on the Kingdom of Christ.

The great meditation on the Two Standards returns us to a thoroughly Augustinian theology of history with its version of the rival camps of Christ and Satan struggling to dominate the world. In *The Golden Legend* we read of Augustine that his *City of God* had precisely this object: to delineate the cities of Babylon and Jerusalem, the character of the love that inflames the city of Babylon and that which animates the holy city of Jerusalem. In Babylon self-love mounts to contempt of God, while in Jerusalem love of God culminates in contempt of, or disregard for self. The Augustinian phrase is heard again in the Ignatian colloquy which seeks the grace to bear insults and wrongs in imitation of the Divine Majesty, and in the note attached to the Three Classes of Men. His favorite saint, Onuphrius, adds a detail to the meditation on the Two Standards, for in his life, as related in *The Golden Legend*, he refers to Satan as the "enemy of the human race."

It is clear then that even during the period of conversion many of the fundamental themes of the Exercises were already in the mind of Ignatius. But it would need the silence, prayer, and penance of the cave of Manresa to develop them. Father Almares, a close friend of Ignatius, tells us that when Ignatius left for Montserrat and Manresa his soul was already preoccupied with the two basic meditations. The chivalrous nobleman, the spirited soldier, was to give his own particular imprint to the themes he borrowed. At Manresa he learned that the nobility who follow Christ most closely should also wear Christ's livery, namely, contempt of the world, of riches, of a great name among men. The battles described in the Two Standards and the Kingdom are fought out on the field of each individual soul, for the conquest of self-love through love of Christ. While the ancient tradition that the Virgin Mary dictated the Spiritual Exercises to St. Ignatius in the cave of Manresa may be without proof, there can be no doubt that the inspirations of the Holy Spirit were responsible for the final form which Ignatius gave to his little book.

The Exercises follow a closely logical scheme of meditations and contemplations designed to bring the soul closer to the spirit of the two fundamental Exercises of the Kingdom and the Two Standards. The first week is intended to enable the soul to purify itself from false principles and inordinate attachments in order to hear the call of Christ the King and to enter the battle under His standard, while living up to the high standards Ignatius set for a soldier of Christ. The central figure in this week is Christ the Savior, Who invites the one making the Exercises to reform his life according to the principles of Christ. If the exercitant does not show aptitude for proceeding beyond an ordinary good Christian life he should not be given the Exercises of the second week but should end his retreat here, with a good confession and practical reform of life. If, however, he seems likely to profit by making the whole four weeks, then he may be led on by his director to a further exploration of the implications of the Kingdom and the Two Standards, through a study of the Public Life, the Passion, and the Risen Life of Christ.

What ideal end did Ignatius have in mind for the Spiritual Exercises as a whole? Commentators differ widely in their expression of the end and purpose of the Exercises. It seems clear that one immediate end is to discover God's will for the disposition of one's life, for example: should one embrace a particular state of life, such as the religious life, or the married state? But the purpose of the Exercises is actually much broader than this. The choice or "election" upon which Ignatius lays such stress applies not only to a state of life but to *anything* that pertains to progress in sanctity. If the purpose of the Exercises was only to determine a state of life, those whose state was already determined, such as clerics, religious, the married, could hardly profit by them. A more general end is service of the Church, learning in all things to love and to serve Jesus Christ and so to attain salvation and happiness. By imitating Jesus Christ and conforming our life to His principles we will avoid undue attachments to people, places, and things that might otherwise hinder our spiritual progress and we will grow in that most necessary of virtues, love of God and our fellow men, in a word, we will grow in sanctity.

The Exercises, as St. Ignatius conceived them, were intended to be useful to many classes of people but they were especially directed at *more* generous souls from whom *greater* service and love of God might be hoped. If one follows the spirituality of the Exercises generously he will be led to sanctity, even to the heights of evangelical perfection. Many, in fact, who made the Exercises under Ignatius' direction, became gifted with mystical prayer and almost continual union with God. This, however, was not the specific aim of Ignatius. His goal was that of an apostolic spirit of generous service, a life of sanctity penetrated by prayer and supporting and evoking it. rather than a spirituality purely contemplative or mystical in its orientation.

The Spiritual Exercises touch on so many important aspects of the spiritual life that they may justly be called a summary of the most profound principles of ascetical theology. Marked as they are with a deep concern for apostolic service of the Church through complete conformity to the will of God. they contain practical principles to arrive at it, some of which are positive and some of which are negative. The central positive principle is the imitation of Christ our Lord, the exemplary cause of all Christian perfection. But to achieve such imitation requires the destruction of egotism, pride, and worldly attachments.

Since the principal obstacle to a soul's perfection is usually made evident through an inordinate attachment to creatures, St. Ignatius proposes that the retreat master school the exercitant in unselfishness. self-conquest. and detachment from finite things, whether material possessions or spiritual ones, such as honor, glory, power. He will then be disposed to make use of creatures only insofar as they lead him to God. This moderation will find its expression in their use, where they lead one to his final end. God, and in their abstention when they do not; it will guide one in contemplating the divine perfections reflected in them. St. Ignatius lays great stress on this practical disposition of soul which he calls "indifference" since it is an absolute practical prerequisite for genuine, realistic progress in the spiritual life. Indifference, however, in Ignatius's thought, is not a kind of baptized stoicism but a straightforward honest love of God which makes us alert to choose whatever will lead us to Him. It is characteristic of Ignatius' plan of development that indifference is demanded of the exercitant from the very beginning of the Exercises. Ignatius has no intention of fostering illusions.

Many books have been written about the essentials of the Ignatian method or Ignatian spirituality. What is meant by it can be seen rather clearly through careful study of the annotations and rules which St. Ignatius provides as a guide to the one giving the Exercises. Consequently one cannot really call a retreat "Ignatian" unless certain essential conditions are faithfully fulfilled. Thus, the exercitant must be active, for passivity is impossible in this type of retreat. Perfect silence must be maintained, *or the retreat cannot be called Ignatian*, no matter how closely the book of the Exercises is otherwise followed. Constant observance of the movements of the soul must be practiced by the exercitant, and prayer for grace must be frequent. Moreover, unless the director explains the additions and rules for each week, and stresses the essential movement of the soul from indifference through compunction to devotion to Christ, contemplation of His mysteries, reform of life and union, and familiarity with God, we cannot speak of the retreat as "Ignatian." But a retreat would not be Ignatian either, if it consisted in a mere parroting of the text, for Ignatius intended it to be a guide book of fundamental principles and points which are to be developed by the director. Only the director who has grasped the mind and heart of Ignatian spirituality, which is *distinguished* service of Christ, can fulfill his task of adapting the Exercises to the precise needs of the individual or group to whom he is speaking. No little skill is required for this work and it presupposes that the director of the retreat is specially fitted for it. An experienced retreat master, who knows the Exercises well, will make numerous little adjustments in his approaches to the meditations to fit the education, temperament, role in life, age bracket, and interests of his audience. This does not imply the omission of essential or key meditations of his own choice but a flexible use of the suggestions and sketches proposed by St. Ignatius.

The same basic ideas of detachment from honors and worldly goods, of close following of Christ's ideals in humility and generous service apply to lay people as well as to religious, and the meditations should be adapted to show this. One obviously would not. for example. propose at a married men's retreat that the exercitants consider the advisability of choosing a more perfect state, e.g., celibacy. but rather that they consider how to perfect themselves in the state they are already in and how to acquire the virtues proper to that state.

Overadaptation is likely to produce a retreat that is simply not Ignatian This would be the case if one were to omit the central meditations of the Kingdom. the Two Standards, the Contemplation to Obtain Divine Love. But, since the original meditations as we have them from the hand of St. Ignatius are so brief and concise, there is ample room for the director of the retreat. after evaluating the spiritual state of the group he is addressing their character and needs, to accommodate these to the situation. Obviously this should be done with tact and prudence. The director is not to substitute personal ideas or personal preferences for the original scheme of meditations. but instead to enrich those chosen by Ignatius, developing them, giving them an orientation specifically suited to his audience.

Without a knowledge of ascetical theology and of human nature as well, he will not be able to do this. But his experiences should give him the sharpness to discern exactly where emphasis should be placed and what amount of time should be spent in each section of the retreat. He must, moreover, exert himself to note the various movements of grace in his audience. to be as close as possible to them that he may observe their progress, to judge their reactions and to follow, insofar as prudence, docility to the Spirit. and the gift of counsel allow, the inspiration that the Spirit is communicating to the individual or to the entire group.

The Holy Spirit is the prime retreat master; the director is only His docile instrument. Consequently he should be skilled in guiding souls, in judging motives and reactions, in assessing personal reactions. The classical spiritual art of discerning spirits, i.e., of judging the signs to indicate what God is suggesting to a soul, is extremely important here and it is an art learned primarily through familiarity with His ways. The resources and discoveries of modern psychology can also be called upon to help the director understand the exercitant, provided, of course, that the director possesses a knowledge of them. But he must constantly seek the guidance of the Holy Spirit to assist him in molding and shaping his talks to achieve the particular emphasis needed by his retreatants.

The role of the director of the Exercises is so important that the question inevitably arises: is it possible for an individual to make the retreat by himself, without the aid of a director? The answer is clear: yes, for many Jesuit priests do precisely this for their annual retreat. They are presumed to be so familiar with the Exercises as to be able to pursue them without outside direction. But the case of a lay person would be quite different. The Exercises do call for a director and it is difficult to conceive an ideal situation where a lay person could do without one.

Laymen and laywomen who decide to make an Ignatian retreat usually do so at a retreat house under the direction of a retreat master. It is his office to have a greater knowledge of the Exercises than could be gained through a simple perusal of this small book. He must understand the meaning hidden deep in the words of the text as well as the inner force and interconnection of each meditation, and have studied Ignatius' ideas with such thoroughness as to have penetrated the saint's mind. The layman is usually not in a position to bring to his study of the Exercises a knowledge of the traditions that surround them and the theological principles which they involve.

However, since it is not always possible for lay people to make a retreat under ideal conditions, in a retreat house equipped with skilled directors, and yet wish to make an Ignatian retreat, we can visualize the expedient of a private retreat based upon the Exercises and "auto-directed." Meditation books exist which develop at great length the points Ignatius sketches, and there are commentaries by scholars who have devoted a lifetime of study to the Exercises.[2] It is conceivable, therefore, that by using the Spiritual Exercises, in conjunction with a standard commentary and a book which amplifies Ignatius' points, the layman could approximate an Ignatian retreat.

The situation however would hardly be ideal. The book of Exercises is essentially a work book, not intended for "spiritual reading" or rapid reading and so schematic that it requires to be fleshed out. Moreover a successful retreat according to this method demands scrupulous attention to the rules set down by St. Ignatius, and an understanding of them, in depth, is hard to come by. Not every cleric, nor every Jesuit has the capability or the training to give a satisfactory retreat. It is much less likely that lay people will have a background required to adapt, develop, and penetrate the often brief suggestions which St. Ignatius has left us.

Since the Spiritual Exercises form the framework of so many annual retreats for priests, religious, and laity, it may be helpful to view them in the light of the criticism of an eminent historian.

Dom John Chapman, in the *Downside Review*, XLVIII (1930), pp. 4–18, stated the case against the annual Ignatian retreat with disturbing forcefulness. In his opinion the meditations, the forming of pictures in the imagination, the application of the senses to be carried out in the course of the popular eight days' retreat according to approved Ignatian methods, fail of their effect after the retreatant has performed them once. "What St. Ignatius meant for once in a lifetime is given year by year to the same people; the preacher follows the Exercises partially and distantly; he tries to interest or startle by introducing new matter; the month is reduced to a week; the choice of a vocation is omitted."

---

[2] Among books in English which give developments of the meditation of the Exercises the following may prove helpful: Aloysius Ambruzzi, *The Spiritual Exercises of St. Ignatius made easier*, London, 1937; Alexander Brou, *The Ignatian Way to God*, Bruce, Milwaukee, 1952; Francis X. McMenamy, *An Eight-Day Retreat based on the Spiritual Exercises of St. Ignatius*, Bruce, Milwaukee, 1956; G. Longhaye, *An Eight-Day Retreat*, Kenedy, New York, 1928.

It would seem to Dom Chapman that the principal good to be obtained from such a repetition of the Spiritual Exercises would flow from the silence enjoined on the retreatants rather than from any efficacy peculiar to the Ignatian meditations and their characteristic concatenation.

For lay people unfamiliar with the system, such a retreat might. he feels, be very useful, if the "sermons were theological and instructive, but for more advanced individuals it is simply dispiriting. "Beginners find the Ignatian method striking· they repeat with less success, and yet again with none at all . . ." From the clearly satisfactory results obtained with beginners of good will. it is tempting to engage in ". . . the businesslike method. human effort cooperating with grace . . . the royal road to sanctity! But it only answers up to a point, and stops dead."

The reasons suggested for this failure on the part of the Exercises seem logical ones at first inspection. What would appear to be operative here is the law of diminishing returns which holds especially for the meditations based upon imaginative and emotional appeal When material has once become familiar. the imagination finds it increasingly difficult to form new and vivid images the emotions are correspondingly slow to respond This might indicate that while St. Ignatius was absolutely right in planning his elaborate system of meditation for unconverted Christians, leading them from the Foundation and their relation to the Creator through the history of their Redemption to the Contemplation on the love of God. his method would not be effective for more advanced Christians. The synthesis might fail once it has become merely a course of sermons preached to the more spiritually advanced, however beautiful it remains in these adaptations.

In point of fact, as Chapman points out, it was not until the time of Father Roothaan, the twenty-first General of the Society of Jesus, that this method began to be taught as the best for all, including the most advanced. This conviction of Father Roothaan, we may note in passing, appears to be echoed in Pope Pius XI's *Mens Nostra*, which calls the book of the Exercises "a most wise and universal code of laws for

the direction of souls in the way of salvation and perfection
. . . showing the way to secure amendment of morals and
. . . the summit of the spiritual life. . . ."

In answer to the objections of Dom John Chapman
we might observe first that it is abundantly clear from St.
Ignatius' letters that he intended his Exercises also for those
who aimed at perfection. This same view of the Exercises is
found to be that of St. Ignatius' close companions, Polanco
and Nadal.

If the immediate end of the Exercises is to be the choice
of a state of life, an ultimate end is certainly the greater glory
of God according to the individual vocation of each retreatant. Such has been the traditional viewpoint of many students
of the Exercises, although some have laid special emphasis on
preparation for the apostolic life, the cultivation of the
presence of God, and divine union in prayer as principal ends.
The latest distinguished interpreter of the Exercises, Father
Pinard de la Boullaye, has given us a complete and authorita-
tive discussion of the various purposes which they may have
in a given situation. He has outlined the adaptations necessary to fit them to those purposes and exemplified his doctrine in three volumes of Ignatian meditations designed for
people who have made the Exercises once or many times.
(*Exercises Spirituels*, Paris, Beauchesne, 1944.)

Obviously, a retreat given to a religious of many years'
standing has a different purpose from one given to a layman,
for example, who is trying to come to a decision about a state
of life. Moreover, the principal good of any Ignatian retreat
is not one which can be derived merely from eight days of
silence. That the retreat master should avoid lengthy sermons
has been stressed too often to demand restatement. His
function is to provide material for meditation, to develop it,
but not to preach. He is expected to interest by molding a
flexible system of meditations to the actual situation of his
hearers. The wealth of his theological and philosophical
science, his knowledge of human nature, and his experience
in the spiritual life are channeled through a set of meditations psychologically adaptable to every age and condition of
man.

For the cleric or religious, the married man or woman, the election of a state of life would be absurd. For such a one the annual retreat serves instead to renew the interior life conformably to the spirit of his or her individual vocation. With this in mind the past year is reviewed and the future year anticipated.

The spiritual losses and gains of the past year are meditated on in order that the *fundamental attitudes* underlying the faults and failures may be discovered and altered. The soul itself is in readiness for a *metanoia*, a new conversion. The corrosive dust of routine is to be blown away, a new understanding sought of the less obviously false principles around which a multitude of apparently disparate faults tends to cluster. A freshness of vision is aimed at by which spiritual truths are reappreciated so that the soul may judge easily and aptly of the relationship of creatures to God, as though by a supernatural instinct. Spiritual principles will then become operative in a special way as they apply to the problems of the individual retreatant.

The insights into spiritual principles gained in prayer and their application to the individual are turned upon the past to discover the fundamental orientations that account for its failures. Motivational forces that have acted upon the retreatant in the year gone by are thus discerned. In the course of a year hundreds of human experiences, of special graces received from God, have altered and reshaped the person making the retreat. External circumstances, interior movements, new influences, persons, places, occupations have offered challenges which have been met successfully or less successfully. These have revealed new tendencies and called out new aspirations which were not so clearly seen before since there was no occasion to actuate them. The daily and vehement press of external activity left little time during the year for long-range evaluation of these new elements in the subject's spiritual life. Now, however, the opportunity is offered for an undisturbed weighing of all these factors; the fruit will be greater knowledge of the self in its process of deification.

That the same regulative principles are offered to the retreatants to help them in their work is scarcely surprising. Were one to discover an entirely new set of directive meditations for such a work, it would be astonishing indeed. The human personality has been "in process" during the year; human nature has remained unchanged.

The Ignatian retreat always looks to the past but with the future in mind. What is God's plan for the individual during the year to come? This is the principal preoccupation of the intellect during the retreat. The holiness that results from the realization of God's designs is the aim of the retreat and this must first be clearly understood. But the plan of God for every individual, which in His mind is possessed as a unit, is revealed only gradually and progressively. As growth takes place in the spiritual life there occurs also a shifting of emphasis in the struggle to achieve perfection. Attitudes of mind and soul for which the individual once strove have now been integrated into the personality, lighting up new decisions to be taken, new approaches to be made. With this deeper understanding of the mind of Christ, the unique exemplary cause of our perfection, there arise new spiritual problems. A simplification takes place of what might be called the mechanics of asceticism, prayer, the imitation of Christ, with one or another aspect of Christ's perfection gradually informing the entire supernatural life, giving new meaning to single virtues, uniting various spiritual efforts under one dynamic principle, one moving intuition.

All these alterations demand a reconsideration of what God demands for the forthcoming year. But the hasty calculation of human prudence is not enough to enlighten the mind in so important a matter. Consequently, the retreatant is expected to do more than listen attentively to a course of sermons and to draw some practical conclusions. He is expected to meditate, to co-operate actively, disposing his mind to receive the intimations of the Holy Spirit, which it may be added, will not always seem as "logical" as the conclusion of a syllogism. The Ignatian retreat is essentially a time of work, not of quiescent silence. It offers in its orderly progression of meditations the means for the exercitant to prepare himself to receive light and to activate his will to accept God's challenge for the period ahead. It presents skillfully planned and graduated motives to the will by its representation of Christ in the Contemplations. But no retreat master can turn these motives into automatic forces for the individual; to become such they must acquire subjective appeal that only the individual's own effort and God's grace can give them.

In the Ignatian retreat the retreatant is brought into contact with "the mind that was in Christ, Jesus" as it is revealed in the mysteries of His life. The personal appeal of the living model that is Christ, motivates the will to unburden itself of whatever has weighed down its *élan* in the past. The transforming effect of such a dwelling with Christ in prayer is able to move the will to initiate decisions necessary for the future. New perceptions of Christ's attitudes and new motives for action are integrated into the personal synthesis of the spiritual life which the retreatant had achieved in past retreats. The resolves he makes now are not so many isolated decisions to be carried out independently of one another or of decisions he has made in the past but are inserted into his already existing spiritual background. From the accumulated force of this background they draw a strength which they could not have in isolation. In turn, these new insights these new motives, reinforce the old motives, the old decisions. Since a vital process always presupposes much self-activity in collaborating with God, it is clear that the use of the same general plan of meditations each year to guide the process, would be deadening only on the supposition that no real changes of any sort have taken place in the individual. But this is an impossibility. To remain stationary, as St. Francis de Sales has remarked, is itself a change in the spiritual life.

The praise that has been lavished upon the Exercises by all manner of men takes into account their nature as an instrument. They are expected to be used; the retreatant can be the principal actuator of their potentialities. The retreat master follows a logically compelling order in his topics for meditation but the chief work remains that of the exercitant co-operating with God's grace.

It is the exercitant who stirs his intelligence to grasp the truths anew, to penetrate to his own basic problems, to take the viewpoint of Christ in all things. It is he who energizes his will with Christ always in view, to take decisive resolutions. If the Ignatian retreat were a course of sermons the retreatant's part would be different. But they are not, and as a result, passivity is entirely out of place. Contemplation of the life of Christ is less a search for new and vivid images than an interior relishing of the movements of the Heart of Christ manifest in His life.

The means necessary for such re-energizing of the spiritual life are obvious. The one making the retreat should sever himself from ordinary occupations and preoccupations allowing himself to be absorbed by Christ, to live in the atmosphere of Christ's life. Silencing the memory, the imagination, the impulses of the heart, where these do not help the work of absorption in Christ, is a primary necessity. Such a silence frees the soul for prayer and disposes it to accept the suave influence of the Holy Spirit enlightening the mind as to God's demands, fortifying the will to strong decision, molding the heart's affections after the model of the Heart of Christ. Only this kind of co-operation with grace will result in the greater glory of God, according to the individual vocation of the retreatant.

TRANSLATOR'S NOTE

The notebook in which St. Ignatius made the original draft of the Spiritual Exercises was lost, or possibly destroyed by the saint himself. The oldest text in existence is the *Autograph* of 1541, made by a member of the Society. St. Ignatius himself made use of this copy, corrected it, and made additions to it. The colotype edition of this text, made in 1908, together with the Latin text of John Roothaan, S.J. (*Exercitia Spiritualia Sancti Patris Ignatii de Loyola*, Madrid, 1920), served as the primary sources of the present translation.

Ignatius did not intend this work to be a literary masterpiece but rather a solid working tool for those who wished to enter into the serious work of their salvation. The structure of the text is sometimes involved and the language abbreviated, but the thought is precise and clear. In order to maintain intact the ideas of Ignatius, we have modified the language and structure only to the point that we considered necessary for clear comprehension by the modern reader. We have made two additions not found in the text of the *Autograph:* to aid in making cross references we have used the marginal paragraph numbers that have become standard since the Marietti Spanish-Latin edition (Turin 1908). We have also included the prayer "Anima Christi" at the beginning of the text. Although this prayer does not appear in the *Autograph*, St. Ignatius uses it on several occasions to close the meditations. It is usual therefore to include it in modern editions as an introductory prayer.

Since this present work is meant for those who wish to make the Exercises or to gain an active knowledge of them, footnotes and explanations have been kept to a minimum. The scholar or those who wish to make a deeper study of the Exercises have excellent commentaries available to them.

Among those that have been consulted for the interpretations in this translation are the Spanish text of José Calveras, S.J. (*Ejercicios Espirituales, Directorio y Documentos,* Barcelona, 1944), the excellent work of Father Jaime Nonell, S.J. (*Los Ejercicios en si mismos y en su Aplicacion,* Manresa, 1896), and the English texts of Aloysius Ambruzzi, S.J. (*The Spiritual Exercises of St. Ignatius,* Mangalore, 1941) and Joseph Rickaby, S.J. (*The Spiritual Exercises of St. Ignatius Loyola, in Spanish and English, with a Continuous Commentary,* New York, 1923).

As an added assistance to those who may wish to use this text to make the Exercises we have included in an appendix the scriptural passages recommended by St. Ignatius for the meditations on the Life of Christ. We have taken these passages from the Confraternity of Christian Doctrine translation of the New Testament.

THE SPIRITUAL EXERCISES OF
St. Ignatius

ANIMA CHRISTI

Soul of Christ, sanctify me.
Body of Christ, save me.
Blood of Christ, inebriate me.
Water from the side of Christ, wash me.
Passion of Christ, strengthen me.
O good Jesu, hear me;
Within Thy wounds hide me;
Suffer me not to be separated from Thee;
From the malignant enemy defend me;
In the hour of my death call me,
And bid me come to Thee,
That with Thy Saints I may praise Thee
For ever and ever. Amen.

DIRECTIONS[1] FOR ACQUIRING AN UNDERSTANDING OF THE SPIRITUAL EXERCISES THAT FOLLOW AND THUS ASSISTING BOTH THOSE WHO ARE TO GIVE THEM AND THOSE WHO MAKE THEM

1. This expression "Spiritual Exercises" embraces every method of examination of conscience, of meditation, of contemplation, of vocal and mental prayer, and of other spiritual activity that will be mentioned later. For just as strolling, walking, and running are bodily exercises, so spiritual exercises are methods of preparing and disposing the soul to free itself of all inordinate attachments, and after accomplishing this, of seeking and discovering the Divine Will regarding the disposition of one's life, thus insuring the salvation of his soul.

2. The one who is giving instruction in the method and procedure of meditation or contemplation should be explicit in stating the subject matter for the contemplation or meditation. He should limit his discourse to a brief, summary statement of its principal points; for then the one who is making the contemplation, by reviewing the true essentials of the subject, and by personal reflection and reasoning may find something that will make it a little more meaningful for him or touch him more deeply. This may happen as a result of his own reasoning or through the enlightenment of his understanding by Divine grace. This is a greater spiritual satisfaction and produces more fruit than if the one who is giving the Exercises were to discourse at great length and amplify the meaning of the subject matter, for it is not an abundance of knowledge that fills and satisfies the soul but rather an interior understanding and savoring of things.

[1] The Spanish term used is *annotaciones*. It is clear from the nature of the first twenty points that they were meant as preliminary instructions for those giving and making the Exercises.

3. As is true in all of the following Spiritual Exercises, one uses the intellect for reasoning while the will is employed in giving expression to the affections. We should realize that in acts of the will, when we are speaking vocally or mentally with God our Lord or His saints, more reverence is required of us than when the intellect is used for reasoning.

4. Four weeks are assigned to the following Spiritual Exercises, corresponding to the four parts into which they are divided: the first, which is the consideration and contemplation of sin; the second, the life of our Lord Jesus Christ up to and including Palm Sunday; the third, the passion of Christ our Lord; and the fourth, the Resurrection and Ascension, to which are appended Three Methods of Prayer. This does not mean that each week must cover seven full days. It may happen that some exercitants are slower than others in finding the contrition, sorrow, and tears for their sins that they are seeking. In like manner some may be more diligent than others, or be more disturbed or tried by different spirits. It may be necessary sometimes to shorten the week and on other occasions to lengthen it. The same is true for the following weeks. The time should be set according to the needs of the subject matter. However, the Exercises should be completed in about thirty days.

5. Anyone making the Exercises will benefit greatly if he enters into them with great courage and generosity with his Creator and Lord, offering Him his entire will, that His Divine Majesty may make use of his person and all that he possesses in accordance with His most holy will.

6. When the one who is giving the Exercises feels that the soul of the exercitant is experiencing neither consolation nor desolation nor any other spiritual movement, or that he has not been troubled by different spirits, he should question him closely about the Exercises; whether he is making them at the appointed time, and in what manner he makes them. He should question him also as to whether he is following the additional directions attentively, and he should require a detailed account of each of these points. Consolation and Desolation are treated on page 129. The additional directions are given on page 60.

7. If the master of the Exercises sees that the exercitant is in desolation or tempted, he should be careful not to be severe or harsh with him but rather gentle and kind. He should give him courage and strength for the future, helping him to see the wiles of the enemy of our human nature, and having him prepare and dispose himself for consolation to come.

8. If the one who is giving the Exercises perceives a need for instruction on the part of the exercitant regarding desolation and the snares of the enemy, as also with respect to consolation, he may explain to him the rules of the first and second week on the discernment of spirits.

9. It is well to observe that when the exercitant is making the Exercises of the first week, if he is a person not well versed in spiritual matters and is tempted strongly and openly, for example, by being shown the obstacles to his further advancement in the service of our Lord, such as, hardships or shame or fear for his worldly honor, etc., then the one giving the Exercises should not talk with him on the rules for discerning different spirits, which are found in the second week. This matter is too subtle and too advanced for him to comprehend, and is likely to do him as much harm as the rules of the first week are likely to be of assistance to him.

10. When the one giving the Exercises feels that the exercitant is being attacked and tempted under the appearance of good, then it would be well to speak with him about the rules of the second week just mentioned. It is more usual for the enemy of our human nature to tempt under the appearances of good when a person is exercising himself in the illuminative way, which corresponds to the Exercises of the second week, and not so much in the purgative way, corresponding to the Exercises of the first week.

11. It is preferable that the person making the Exercises of the first week know nothing of what is to be done in the second week. He should rather work in the first week to acquire what he is seeking, as though he no longer expected to find any good in the second.

12. The one giving the Exercises should impress upon the exercitant that since he must devote one hour to each of the

five Exercises or contemplations that are to be made each
day, that he should always be completely satisfied in his
conscience that he has spent a full hour at the Exercise. It is
better to spend even more than an hour rather than less; since
the enemy frequently tries to have us shorten the hour for
such contemplation, meditation, or prayer.

13. It should be noted also that just as in time of consolation it is simple and easy to remain in contemplation for an
entire hour, so it is quite difficult in time of desolation to
complete the hour. Therefore, to fight against desolation and
to conquer temptation, the exercitant should continue a little
beyond the full hour. Thus he will accustom himself not only
to resist the adversary, but even to vanquish him completely.

14. If the one who is giving the Exercises sees that the
exercitant is making them very fervently and in consolation,
he should advise him and admonish him against making any
hasty or unconsidered promise or vow. The more aware he
is of the exercitant's fickleness of character the more he should
warn and admonish him. Even though one may rightfully
urge another to embrace the religious life, where it is understood that he will take vows of obedience, poverty, and chastity, and although a good work done under vow is more meritorious than one done without vow, still one should consider
carefully the individual circumstances and character of the
person concerned, and what help or obstacles he would meet
in accomplishing what he wishes to promise.

15. The one who gives the Exercises should not encourage
the exercitant to embrace poverty, or to make any other
promise rather than its contrary; neither should he encourage
him to embrace one state of life rather than another. Even
though apart from the Exercises it would be both lawful
and meritorious to urge all who are probably fitted for it to
embrace continence, virginity, religious life, and all other
forms of evangelical perfection, in these Spiritual Exercises
it is much better and more fitting in seeking the Divine
Will, that our Lord and Savior should communicate Himself to the devout soul, inflaming it with His love and praise,
and disposing it to the way in which it can best serve Him in
the future. Thus, the one who gives the Exercises should not

lean either to one side or the other, but standing in the middle like the balance of a scale, he should allow the Creator to work directly with the creature, and the creature with its Creator and God.

16. In order that the Creator and Lord may work more surely in His creature, if such soul has any inordinate inclinations or attachments, it will be most useful for it to work as forcefully as possible to attain the contrary of that to which the present attachment tends. For instance, if a soul is inclined to seek or keep some office or benefice, not for the honor and glory of God our Lord nor for the salvation of souls, but for its personal convenience and temporal gain, the soul must change the direction of its affections. By earnest prayer and other spiritual exercises it must ask the contrary of God our Lord. That is to say it should desire to have no such office or benefice, nor anything else, unless the Divine Majesty, restoring order to the soul's wishes change its first desire, so that now the reason for desiring or holding such office or benefice is solely the service, the honor, and the glory of God.

17. The one giving the Exercises need not inquire into, nor know the personal thoughts and sins of the one who is making the Exercises, but it will be very useful for him to be kept faithfully informed of the various disturbances and thoughts which the different spirits awaken in him. In this way, depending on whether the exercitant progresses little or much, the director can give the spiritual exercises most in conformity with the needs of his soul.

18. The Spiritual Exercises should be adapted to the requirements of the persons who wish to make them, that is to say, according to their age, their education and their aptitudes. A person who is uneducated or of little natural ability should not be given matter which he could not conveniently bear or from which he could get no profit. In like manner to each should be given those exercises which will be of the most profit to him depending on his disposition and the amount of progress he wishes to make. Thus one who wishes to be helped only to get instruction and to reach a certain degree of spiritual contentment, may be given the

Particular Examination of Conscience (page 48) and afterwards the General Examination of Conscience, (page 50) together with the Method of Prayer on the Commandments, the Deadly Sins, etc., for a half hour in the morning. Weekly confession of his sins is also to be recommended, and if possible, Holy Communion every two weeks, or better, if he is so inclined, every week. This method of giving the Exercises is best suited to those who are illiterate or poorly educated: each commandment should be explained, and also the Deadly Sins, the precepts of the Church, the uses of the five senses, and the Works of Mercy.

If the director of the Exercises sees that the exercitant has little aptitude, or little natural ability or that he is one from whom little fruit could be expected, it is better to give him some of the easier exercises until he has gone to confession, and then to give him some methods of examination of conscience and a program for more frequent confession than has been his custom, so that he may preserve what he has gained, without going further into the matter of the election[2] nor into any other exercises beyond those of the first week, especially when greater profit may be gained with others, since there is insufficient time for everything.

19. A person engaged in public affairs or necessary business, if he is educated and has ability, can make the Exercises by taking an hour and a half for them each day. First, the end for which man is created should be explained to him, then he can also be given the Particular Examination of Conscience for half an hour; and afterwards the General Examination of Conscience and also the method of confessing and of receiving the Blessed Sacrament. He can make each morning for three days, one hour of meditation on the first, second, and third sins (page 54). For three more days, at the same hour, the meditation should be a review of his sins (page 56). Three more days, at the same hour, he should meditate on the punishment due to sin (page 59).

---

[2] The Spanish term *eleccion* is used by St. Ignatius to refer to the choice of a way of life, or a manner of living. The manner of making this choice is found in the Exercises of the second week.

With all three meditations he should be given the Ten Additional Directions (page 60). He should use the method described in the following Exercises for meditation on the mysteries of Christ our Lord.

20. One who is not involved in worldly affairs and who wishes to make the greatest possible progress, should be given all the Spiritual Exercises in the manner in which they are here set forth. In these Exercises, as a general rule, he will profit all the more if he is separated from all of his friends and from all worldly cares; for example, if he moves from the house where he lives and chooses another home or room where he may dwell as privately as possible, so that he may be free to go to Mass and Vespers every day, without fear of hindrance from his friends. There are three principal advantages, among many others to be gained by such seclusion: the first is that the person who withdraws from many friends and acquaintances and from distracting temporal concerns, in order to serve and praise God our Lord, gains no little merit from His Divine Majesty. The second is that being thus separated, not having his mind divided by many things but giving all his care to only one, which is the service of his Creator and the profiting of his own soul, he is more at liberty to use his natural ability in searching more diligently for what he desires so strongly. The third advantage is that the more the soul finds itself alone and away from men, the more apt it is to approach and be united with its Creator and Lord. The closer the soul approaches Him, the more it is disposed to receive graces and gifts from His divine and sovereign goodness.

FIRST WEEK

PURPOSE OF THE EXERCISES

The purpose of these Exercises is to help the exercitant to conquer himself, and to regulate his life so that he will not be influenced in his decisions by any inordinate attachment.

PRESUPPOSITION

In order that the one who gives these Exercises and he who makes them may be of more assistance and profit to each other, they should begin with the presupposition that every good Christian ought to be more willing to give a good interpretation to the statement of another than to condemn it as false. If he cannot give a good interpretation to this statement, he should ask the other how he understands it, and if he is in error, he should correct him with charity. If this is not sufficient, he should seek every suitable means of correcting his understanding so that he may be saved from error.

PRINCIPLE AND FOUNDATION

Man is created to praise, reverence, and serve God our Lord, and by this means to save his soul. All other things on the face of the earth are created for man to help him fulfill the end for which he is created. From this it follows that man is to use these things to the extent that they will help him to attain his end. Likewise, he must rid himself of them in so far as they prevent him from attaining it.

Therefore we must make ourselves indifferent to all created things, in so far as it is left to the choice of our free will and is not forbidden. Acting accordingly, for our part, we should not prefer health to sickness, riches to poverty, honor to dishonor, a long life to a short one, and so in all things we should desire and choose only those things which will best help us attain the end for which we are created.

PARTICULAR EXAMINATION OF CONSCIENCE TO BE MADE EVERY DAY

This Exercise is performed at three different times, and there are two examinations to be made.

The first time: As soon as he arises in the morning the exercitant should resolve to guard himself carefully against the particular sin or defect which he wishes to correct or amend.

The second time: After the noon meal he should ask God our Lord for what he desires, namely, the grace to remember how many times he has fallen into the particular sin or defect, and to correct himself in the future. Following this he should make the first examination demanding an account of his soul regarding that particular matter which he proposed for himself and which he desires to correct and amend. He should review each hour of the time elapsed from the moment of rising to the moment of this examination, and he should make note on the first line of the following diagram, a mark for each time that he has fallen into the particular sin or defect. He should then renew his resolution to improve himself until the time of the second examination that he will make.

The third time: After the evening meal he will make a second examination, reviewing each hour from the first examination to this second one, and on to the second line of the same diagram he will again make a mark for each time that he has fallen into the particular sin or defect.

FOUR ADDITIONAL DIRECTIONS

The following directions will help to remove more quickly the particular sin or defect.

G _____

G _____

G _____

G _____

G _____

G _____

G _____

1. Each time that one falls into the particular sin or defect, he should place his hand on his breast, repenting that he has fallen. This can be done even in the presence of many people without their noticing it.

2. Since the first line of the diagram represents the first examination, and the second line, the second examination, at night the exercitant should observe whether there is an improvement from the first line to the second, that is, from the first examination to the second.

3. He should compare the second day with the first, that is to say, the two examinations of the present day with the two examinations of the preceding day, and see if there is a daily improvement.

4. He should also compare one week with another and see if there is a greater improvement during the present week than in the past week. It may be noted that the first large G denotes Sunday. The second is smaller and stands for Monday, the third, for Tuesday, and so forth.

GENERAL EXAMINATION OF CONSCIENCE

To help the exercitant purify himself and make better confessions.

I presuppose that I have three kinds of thoughts in my mind. The first is a thought which is my own and which comes solely from my own liberty and will; the other two come from without, the one from the good spirit and the other from the evil one.

Thoughts: There are two ways of gaining merit from an evil thought which comes from without:

1. The thought comes to me to commit a mortal sin. I resist the thought immediately and it is conquered.

2. When the same evil thought comes to me and I resist it, and it returns again and again, but I continue to resist it until it is vanquished. This second way is much more meritorious than the first.

One is guilty of venial sin if the same thought of committing mortal sin comes to him and he gives it some attention or takes some sensual pleasure in it, or when there is some negligence in rejecting it.

There are two ways of sinning mortally:

The first exists when one consents to an evil thought with the intention of carrying it out later, or with the intention of doing so if he could.

The second way of sinning mortally is to put the thought of the sin into action. This is a more grievous sin for three reasons:

1. Because of the greater length of time.
2. Because of the greater intensity.
3. Because of the greater injury done to both persons.

Sins of words:

One must not swear by the Creator nor by any creature unless it concerns the truth, and unless it be through necessity and with reverence. By necessity I mean, not when any truth at all is affirmed under oath, but when it is of real importance, for the profit of the soul or the body or for the protection of temporal goods. By reverence I mean that one will reflect on the honor and reverence due his Creator and Lord when he uses His name.

It should be noted that when we take an unnecessary oath we sin more seriously if we swear by the Creator than if we swear by a creature. Still, it is more difficult to swear in the proper manner, that is with truth, necessity, and reverence, by a creature than by the Creator, for the following reasons:

1. When we want to swear by some creature, the desire to name the creature does not make us so attentive and prudent in telling the truth, or to consider whether it is necessary to swear, as we would be when we use the name of the Creator and Lord of all things.

2. When we swear by any creature, it is not so easy to show reverence and respect to the Creator as when we swear in the name of the Creator and Lord Himself; for the wish to use the name of God our Lord carries with it a greater respect and reverence than the wish to take an oath in the name of a creature. This is why it is more permissible for those who are perfect than for those who are imperfect to swear by a creature. Due to their continued contemplation and the enlightenment of their understanding, the perfect are more able to consider, meditate, and contemplate God our Lord as existing in all creatures by his essence, presence, and power. Thus, when they swear by a creature they are more likely to be disposed to show respect and reverence for their Creator and Lord than those who are imperfect.

3. In frequently swearing by a creature, idolatry is more to be feared in the imperfect than in the perfect.

Idle words should not be spoken. By idle words I mean words which serve no good purpose, and do not profit me or anyone else, nor are they intended to do so. Words spoken for a useful purpose or words intended for the good of one's soul or that of another, or for the good of the body, or for one's temporal welfare are never idle words. Neither are words idle because one speaks of matters which are foreign to his state, for example, if a religious speaks of wars or of commerce. In all that has been mentioned there is merit if the words are directed to a good end, and it is sinful if they are directed to a bad end, or spoken idly.

Nothing should be said to defame or slander another. If I reveal a hidden mortal sin committed by another, I sin mortally. If I reveal another's hidden venial sin, I sin venially. In revealing the defects of another I thereby make known my own defect. If the intention is good, the defect or sin of another may be spoken of:

1. When the sin is public, as in the case of a woman openly engaged in prostitution, or a sentence passed by a court of justice, or a known error which is corrupting the souls of those with whom we are conversing.

2. When the hidden sin is made known to someone to help him rise from his own sin. There must, however, be some grounds or probable reasons for expecting that this will help him.

Sins of deeds:

The subject matter is the Ten Commandments, the precepts of the Church, and the recommendations of superiors. Any action committed against any of these three groups is a more or less serious sin according to the gravity of the matter. By recommendations of superiors I mean, for example, the Indulgences attached to the Crusade and other Indulgences, such as those for peace, requiring confession and reception of the most Holy Sacrament. For we would not sin lightly if we acted or caused others to act against such pious recommendations and exhortations of superiors.

Method of Making the General Examination of Conscience

This examination contains five points:

1. The first point is to render thanks to God for the favors we have received.

2. The second point is to ask the grace to know my sins and to free myself from them.

3. The third point is to demand an account of my soul from the moment of rising until the present examination; either hour by hour or from one period to another. I shall first make an examination of my thoughts, then my words, and then my actions in the same order as that given in the Particular Examination of Conscience.

4. The fourth point is to ask pardon of God our Lord for my failings.

5. The fifth point is to resolve to amend my life with the help of God's grace. Close with the "Our Father."

GENERAL CONFESSION AND HOLY COMMUNION

Anyone who of his own accord wishes to make a general Confession during the period of the Spiritual Exercises will find, among many other advantages, these three:

1. Although anyone who confesses once a year is not required to make a general confession, by doing so he will gain much more profit and merit because of the greater sorrow he will have for his sins and for the wickedness of his whole life.

2. Just as during the Spiritual Exercises a person gains a more intimate knowledge of his sins and their malice than at a time when he is not occupied with his interior life, so now because of this greater understanding and sorrow for his sins, he will find greater profit and merit than he would have had before.

3. After making a better confession and being better disposed, he will be more worthy and better prepared to receive the most Holy Sacrament, which will help him not only to avoid sin but also to preserve and increase grace.

It would be best to make this general confession immediately after the Exercises of the first week.

THE FIRST EXERCISE

This meditation is made with the three powers of the soul, and the subject is the first, second, and third sins. It contains, the preparatory prayer, two preludes, three principal points, and a colloquy.

Prayer: The purpose of the preparatory prayer is to ask of God our Lord the grace that all my intentions, actions, and works may be directed purely to the service and praise of His Divine Majesty.

The first prelude is a mental image of the place. It should be noted at this point that when the meditation or contemplation is on a visible object, for example, contemplating Christ our Lord during His life on earth, the image will consist of seeing with the mind's eye the physical place where the object that we wish to contemplate is present. By the physical place I mean, for instance, a temple, or mountain where Jesus or the Blessed Virgin is, depending on the subject of the contemplation. In meditations on subject matter that is not visible, as here in meditation on sins, the mental image will consist of imagining, and considering my soul imprisoned in its corruptible body, and my entire being in this vale of tears as an exile among brute beasts. By entire being I mean both body and soul.

The second prelude is to ask God our Lord for what I want and desire. The request must be according to the subject matter. Therefore, if the contemplation is on the Resurrection I shall ask for joy with Christ rejoicing; if it is on the passion, I shall ask for pain, tears, and suffering with Christ suffering. In the present meditation I shall ask for shame and confusion, for I see how many souls have been damned for a single mortal sin, and how often I have deserved to be damned eternally for the many sins I have committed.

NOTE

The preparatory prayer without change, and the two preludes mentioned above, which may be changed at times if the subject matter requires it, are to be made before all contemplations and meditations.

The first point will be to recall to memory the first sin, which was that of the angels, then to apply the understanding by considering this sin in detail, then the will by seeking to remember and understand all, so that I may be the more ashamed and confounded when I compare the one sin of the angels with the many that I have committed. Since they went to hell for one sin, how many times have I deserved it for my many sins. I will recall to mind the sin of the angels, remembering that they were created in the state of grace, that they refused to make use of their freedom to offer reverence and obedience to their Creator and Lord, and so sinning through pride, they fell from grace into sin and were cast from heaven into hell. In like manner my understanding is to be used to reason more in detail on the subject matter, and thereby move more deeply my affections through the use of the will.

The second point is to employ the three powers of the soul to consider the sin of Adam and Eve. Recall to mind how they did such long penance for their sin and what corruption fell upon the whole human race, causing so many to go to hell. I say to recall to mind the second sin, that of our first parents. Recall that after Adam had been created in the Plain of Damascus and placed in the earthly paradise, and Eve had been formed from his rib, they were forbidden to eat the fruit of the tree of knowledge, and eating it they committed sin. After their sin, clothed in garments of skin and cast out of paradise, without the original justice which they had lost, they lived all their lives in much travail and great penance.

The understanding is likewise to be used in considering

the subject matter in greater detail and the will is to be employed as already explained.

The third point is to recall to mind the third sin. This is the particular sin of any person who went to hell because of one mortal sin. Consider also the innumerable others who have gone to hell for fewer sins than I have committed. I say to consider the third particular sin. Recall to mind the grievousness and malice of sin against our Creator and Lord. Let the understanding consider how in sinning and acting against Infinite Goodness, one has justly been condemned forever. Close with acts of the will, as mentioned above.

Colloquy. Imagine Christ our Lord before you, hanging upon the cross. Speak with Him of how, being the Creator He then became man, and how, possessing eternal life, He submitted to temporal death to die for our sins.

Then I shall meditate upon myself and ask "What have I done for Christ? What am I now doing for Christ? What ought I do for Christ?" As I see Him in this condition, hanging upon the cross, I shall meditate on the thoughts that come to my mind.

The colloquy is made properly by speaking as one friend speaks to another, or as a servant speaks to his master, now asking some favor, now accusing oneself for some wrong deed, or again, making known his affairs to Him and seeking His advice concerning them. Conclude with the "Our Father."

THE SECOND EXERCISE

This is a meditation on sin. It consists of the preparatory prayer, two preludes, five points, and a colloquy.

Prayer: This is the same as the first Exercise.

The first prelude is the same as in the first Exercise.

The second prelude is to ask for what I desire. I shall here beg for an ever increasing and intense sorrow and tears for my sins.

The first point is the review of my sins. I shall recall to mind all the sins of my life, looking at them year by year, and period by period. Three things will help me to do this:

first, I shall recall to mind the place and house where I lived; secondly, the associations I have had with others; thirdly, the positions which I have filled.

The second point is to weigh my sins, considering the loathesomeness and the malice that every mortal sin committed has in itself, even though it were not forbidden.

The third point is to consider who I am and abase myself by these examples:

1. What am I in comparison to all men?

2. What are men in comparison with the angels and saints of heaven?

3. What is all creation in comparison with God? Then myself alone, what can I be?

4. Let me consider all my own corruption and foulness of body.

5. Let me see myself as a sore and an abscess from whence have come forth so many sins, so many evils, and the most vile poison.

The fourth point is now to consider who God is against whom I have sinned, recalling his attributes and comparing them to their contraries in me: His wisdom to my ignorance; His omnipotence to my weakness; His justice with my iniquity, His goodness with my sinfulness.

The fifth point is to be struck with amazement and filled with a growing emotion as I consider how creatures have suffered me to live, and have sustained me in life. How the angels, the swords of Divine Justice, tolerated me, guarded me, and prayed for me. How the saints have interceded and prayed for me. How the heavens, moon, and stars, and the elements; fruits, birds, fishes, and animals have all served my needs. How the earth has not opened and swallowed me up, creating new hells that I might suffer eternal torment in them.

Colloquy. I will end this meditation with a colloquy directing my thoughts to God's mercy. I will give thanks to Him for having granted me life until now, and I will resolve with the help of His grace to amend my life for the future. Close with an "Our Father."

THE THIRD EXERCISE

This is a repetition of the first and second Exercises, with three colloquies.

After the preparatory prayer and the two preludes, the first and second Exercises are to be repeated. I will note and dwell upon the points in which I have felt the greatest consolation or desolation, or the greatest spiritual relish. I will then make these colloquies in the following manner.

The first colloquy is with our Lady, that she may obtain grace for me from her Son and Lord for three things:

1. That I may have a thorough knowledge of my sins and a feeling of abhorrence for them.
2. That I may comprehend the disorder of my actions, so that detesting them I will amend my ways and put my life in order.
3. That I may know the world, and being filled with horror of it, I may put away from me worldly and vain things.

Conclude with the "Hail Mary."

The second colloquy is with the Son of God. I will beg Him to intercede with the Father to obtain these graces for me. Conclude with the "Anima Christi."

The third colloquy is with our Eternal Father. I will request that He Himself grant these graces to me. Conclude with the "Our Father."

THE FOURTH EXERCISE

This is a résumé of the third Exercise.

I have called this a résumé because the intellect, without digression, is to recall and review thoroughly the matters contemplated in the previous Exercises. The same three colloquies should then be made.

THE FIFTH EXERCISE

This is a meditation on hell. It contains a preparatory prayer, two preludes, five points, and a colloquy.

Preparatory prayer: This prayer will be as usual.

First prelude: This is the representation of place. Here it will be to see in imagination the length, breadth, and depth of hell.

Second prelude: I will ask for what I desire. Here it will be to ask for a deep awareness of the pain suffered by the damned, so that if I should forget the love of the Eternal Lord, at least the fear of punishment will help me to avoid falling into sin.

First point: To see in imagination the great fires, and the souls enveloped, as it were, in bodies of fire.

Second point: To hear the wailing, the screaming, cries, and blasphemies against Christ our Lord and all His saints.

Third point: To smell the smoke, the brimstone, the corruption, and rottenness.

Fourth point: To taste bitter things, as tears, sadness, and remorse of conscience.

Fifth point: With the sense of touch to feel how the flames surround and burn souls.

Colloquy: Enter into a colloquy with Christ our Lord. Recall to mind the souls in hell, some are there because they did not believe in His coming; others, though they believed, did not act according to His Commandments.

I can divide these souls into three classes:

1. Those who went to hell before the coming of Christ.
2. Those who were damned during His lifetime.
3. Those condemned to hell after His life in the world.

I will now give Him thanks for not having permitted me to fall into any of these classes, thus putting an end to my life.

I will also thank Him for the great kindness and mercy

He has always shown me until this present moment. Conclude with an "Our Father."

NOTE

The first Exercise will be made at midnight; the second, immediately on rising in the morning: the third, before or after Mass but before dinner; the fourth, at the hour of Vespers. It is understood that this arrangement of hours, more or less, is to be observed during the entire four weeks, in so far as age, disposition, and physical constitution enable the exercitant to make five exercises or fewer.

ADDITIONAL DIRECTIONS

To help the exercitant make the Exercises better and to assist him in finding what he desires:

1. After going to bed, as I am about to go to sleep, for the space of a "Hail Mary," I should think of the hour when I have to rise, and for what purpose, summing up the Exercises I have to make.

2. When I wake up, I will not permit my mind to wander to other things, I will turn it at once to the subject that I am going to contemplate in the first Exercise at midnight. I shall be filled with confusion for my many sins, thinking of such examples as that of a knight who finds himself in the presence of his king and the entire court and is filled with shame and confusion for having so greatly offended him from whom he had already received so many gifts and favors.

In like manner, in the second Exercise, I will see myself as a great sinner, bound in chains, who is about to appear before the supreme, eternal Judge; and I will take as an example how prisoners in chains and worthy of death appear before their earthly judge. As I dress I will think over these thoughts, or others, according to the subject matter.

3. A step or two from the place where I am going to meditate or contemplate, I will stand for the space of an "Our Father," and with my mind raised on high, I will consider that God our Lord sees me, etc. And I will make an act of reverence or humility.

4. I will enter into the meditation, at times kneeling, at times prostrate on the ground, at other times supine, or seated or standing, always intent on seeking what I desire. Two things should be noted:

a. If I find what I am seeking while kneeling I will not change my posture, and if prostrate, I will continue in that position, etc.

b. When I find that which I desire, I will meditate quietly, without being anxious to continue further until I have satisfied myself.

5. After I have finished an Exercise I will examine for the space of a quarter of an hour, either while sitting or walking, how I have succeeded in the meditation or contemplation. If I have performed the Exercise poorly, I will seek out the cause, and when I have found it, I will be sorry, so that I may make amends in the future. If I have performed the Exercise well, I will thank God our Lord, and follow the same method next time.

6. I will not think of pleasant and joyful things as heaven, the Resurrection, etc., for such consideration of joy and delight will hinder the feeling of pain, sorrow, and tears that I should have for my sins. It would be better for me to keep in mind that I want to feel sorrow and pain, remembering death and the judgment.

7. For the same reason I will deprive myself of all light, closing the shutters and doors when I am in my room, unless I need the light to say my prayers, to read, or to eat.

8. I will neither laugh nor say anything that will provoke laughter.

9. I will restrain my eyes except in looking to receive or dismiss the person with whom I have to speak.

10. This direction is concerned with penance, which is divided into interior and exterior. Interior penance is sorrow for one's sins, and a firm resolution not to commit them or any others. Exterior penance is the fruit of interior penance, and is the punishment we inflict upon ourselves for the sins committed. We perform this penance in three ways:

a. Regarding food. It will be noted that when we deny ourselves what is superfluous, it is not penance but temperance. It is penance when we deny ourselves what is proper for us to have, and the more we deny ourselves the greater and better is the penance, provided we do not harm ourselves or cause ourselves serious illness.

b. Regarding sleeping. Here again it is not penance when we deny ourselves the superfluity of delicate and soft things. But it is penance when we deny ourselves what is suitable for us. Again, the more we deny ourselves the greater is the penance, provided we cause ourselves no injury or serious illness. Nor should we deny ourselves our due amount of sleep unless we have the bad habit of sleeping too much. It may then be done to arrive at a proper mean.

c. By chastising the flesh, thereby causing sensible pain. This is done by wearing hairshirts, cords, or iron chains on the body, or by scourging or wounding oneself, or by other kinds of austerities.

What seems the most suitable and safest thing in doing penance is for the pain to be felt in the flesh, without penetration to the bones, thus causing pain but not illness. Therefore it seems more fitting to scourge oneself with light cords, which cause exterior pain, than in another way that might cause internal infirmity.

Four Observations on Penance

1. Exterior penances are performed principally to produce three effects:

a. To satisfy for past sins.

b. To overcome ourselves, so that sensuality will be obedient to reason and our lower inclinations be subject to higher ones.

c. To seek and find some grace or gift that we wish to obtain, as for instance, a deep sorrow for our sins, or to grieve for them or for the pains and sufferings that Christ our Lord endured in His passion, or for the solution of some doubt that is troubling us.

2. It is to be noted that the first and second additional directions should be applied to the Exercises at midnight and at daybreak, and not for the Exercises that are made at other times. The fourth direction will never be followed in Church in the presence of others, but only in private, as at home, etc.

3. When the exercitant still does not find what he is seeking, for example, tears, consolations, etc., he will often find it advantageous to change his penance in the matter of food, sleep, or the other acts that he has been performing. Thus we may alternate, doing penance for two or three days, and then for two or three days omitting it. For some it is better to do more penance and for others less. We often fail to do penance also out of love for what pleases the senses and through a false conviction that human nature cannot bear it without notable illness. Sometimes, on the contrary, we may do too much penance, thinking that our body can bear it. Since God our Lord knows our nature infinitely better than we do, often in such changes He grants to each of us to understand what best suits us.

4. The Particular Examination of Conscience will be made to remove defects and negligences relating to the Exercises and the additional directions. This will also be done in the second, third and fourth weeks.

SECOND WEEK

THE KINGDOM OF CHRIST

The call of the earthly king helps us to contemplate the life of the Eternal King.

Prayer: The preparatory prayer will be as usual.

First prelude: This is a mental picture of the place. Here we will see in our imagination the synagogues, villages, and towns where Jesus preached.

Second prelude: I will ask for the grace that I desire. Here it will be to ask of our Lord the grace that I may not be deaf to His call, but prompt and diligent to accomplish His most holy will.

PART ONE

First point: I will see in my mind a human king, chosen by God our Lord Himself, to whom all princes and all Christians pay reverence and obedience.

Second point: I will consider how this king speaks to all his subjects, saying, "It is my will to conquer all infidel lands. Therefore, whoever wishes to come with me must be content to eat as I eat, drink as I drink, dress as I dress, etc. He must also be willing to work with me by day, and watch with me by night. He will then share with me in victory as he has shared in the toils."

Third point: I will consider what the answer of good subjects ought to be to such a generous and noble king, and consequently, if anyone would refuse the request of such a king, how he would deserve to be despised by everyone, and considered an unworthy knight.

PART TWO

The second part of this Exercise consists in applying the example of this earthly king to Christ our Lord, in these three points:

First point: If we heed such a call of an earthly king to his subjects, how much more worthy of consideration is it to see Christ our Lord, the Eternal King, and before Him, all of mankind, to whom, and to each man in particular, He calls and says: "It is My will to conquer the whole world and all My enemies, and thus to enter into the glory of My Father. Whoever wishes to come with Me must labor with Me, so that following Me in suffering, he may also follow Me in glory."

Second point: I will consider that all persons who have judgment and reason will offer themselves completely for this work.

Third point: Those who wish to show the greatest affection and to distinguish themselves in every service of their Eternal King and Universal Lord, will not only offer themselves entirely for the work, but by working against their own sensuality and carnal and worldly love, will make offerings of greater value and importance saying:

Eternal Lord of all things, I make this offering with Thy grace and help, in the presence of Thy infinite goodness and in the presence of Thy glorious Mother and of all the Saints of Thy heavenly court, that it is my wish and desire, and my deliberate choice, provided only that it be for Thy greater service and praise, to imitate Thee in bearing all injuries, all evils, and all poverty both physical and spiritual, if Thy most Sacred Majesty should will to choose me for such a life and state.

OBSERVATIONS

1. This Exercise shall be made twice during the day: in the morning when we rise, and an hour before dinner or supper.

2. It will be very profitable to read some passages from the *Imitation of Christ* or from the Gospels and the *Lives of the Saints*, during the second week and thereafter.

FIRST DAY AND FIRST CONTEMPLATION

This contemplation is on the Incarnation. It contains the preparatory prayer, three preludes, three points, and a colloquy.

Prayer: The usual preparatory prayer.

The first prelude is to recall to mind the history of the subject I am about to contemplate. Here it is how the Three Divine Persons were looking upon the whole extent and space of the earth, filled with human beings. They see that all were going down into hell, and They decreed, in Their eternity, that the Second Person should become man to save the human race. When the fullness of time had come, They sent the Angel Gabriel to our Lady.

The second prelude is a mental representation of the place. I will see, in imagination, the great extent and space of the world, where dwell so many different nations and peoples. I will then see particularly the city of Nazareth in the province of Galilee, and the house and room where our Lady dwells.

The third prelude is to ask for what I desire. Here I will ask for an intimate knowledge of our Lord, who has become man for me, that I may love and follow Him better.

NOTE

It is well to observe here that the same preparatory prayer without change, as was mentioned in the beginning, and the same three preludes, are to be made during this week and the following weeks. The form may be changed when necessary to conform to the subject matter.

The first point. First, I will see all the different people on the face of the earth, so varied in dress and in behavior. Some are white and others black; some at peace and others at war; some weeping and others laughing; some well and others sick; some being born and others dying, etc.

Second, I will see and consider the Three Divine Persons seated on the royal throne of the Divine Majesty. They behold the entire face and extent of the earth and They behold all nations in such great blindness, dying, and going down into hell.

Third, I will see our Lady and the angel who greets her. I will reflect, that I may draw profit from this scene.

The second point. I will hear what the people throughout the world are saying, how they converse with one another, how they swear and blaspheme, etc. I will also listen to what the Three Divine Persons are saying, that is, "Let us work the redemption of mankind," etc. I shall then listen to what the angel and our Lady are saying. I will then reflect upon what I hear to draw profit from their words.

The third point. I will consider what the people throughout the world are doing; how they are wounding, killing, and going to hell, etc. I will also consider what the Three Divine Persons are doing, namely, accomplishing the most Holy Incarnation, etc., also what the angel and our Lady are doing, as the angel fulfills his office of ambassador, and our Lady humbles herself and gives thanks to the Divine Majesty. I will then reflect to derive some profit from each of these things.

The colloquy. I will now think of what I should say to the Three Divine Persons, or the eternal Word Incarnate, or to His Mother and our Lady. I will ask help according to the need that I feel within myself, so that I may more closely follow and imitate our Lord who has just become Incarnate. Close with the "Our Father."

SECOND CONTEMPLATION

The second contemplation is on the Nativity.

Preparatory prayer: The usual prayer.

The first prelude is to review the history of the Nativity. How our Lady, almost nine months with child, set out from Nazareth, seated on an ass, as may piously be believed, together with Joseph and a servant girl leading an ox. They are going to Bethlehem to pay the tribute that Caesar has imposed on the whole land.

The second prelude is to form a mental image of the scene and see in my imagination the road from Nazareth to Bethlehem. I will consider its length and breadth, and whether it is level or winding through valleys and over hills. I will also behold the place of the cave of the Nativity, whether it is large or small, whether high or low, and what it contains.

The third prelude will be the same and in the same form as it was in the preceding contemplation.

The first point is to see the persons: our Lady and St. Joseph, the servant girl, and the Child Jesus after his birth. I will become a poor, miserable, and unworthy slave looking upon them, contemplating them, and ministering to their needs, as though I were present there. I will then reflect within myself in order that I may derive some fruit.

The second point is to observe, consider, and contemplate what they are saying and to reflect within myself that I may derive some profit.

The third point is to observe and consider what they are doing: the journey and suffering which they undergo in order that our Lord might be born in extreme poverty, and after so many labors; after hunger and thirst, heat and cold, insults and injuries, He might die on the cross, and all this for me. I will then reflect in order to gain some spiritual profit.

The colloquy. Conclude with a colloquy as in the preceding contemplation and with the "Our Father."

THIRD CONTEMPLATION

This is a repetition of the first and second Exercises.

After the preparatory prayer and the three preludes, repeat the first and second Exercises. Always make note of some of the more important parts in which one has found some understanding, consolation, or desolation. Conclude in the same manner with a colloquy and the "Our Father."

NOTE

In this repetition and in all those that follow, the same order of procedure will be observed as in the repetition of the first week, changing the subject matter but following the same form.

FOURTH CONTEMPLATION

This is a repetition of the first and second Exercises in the same manner as in the repetition given above.

FIFTH CONTEMPLATION

The purpose of this contemplation will be to apply the five senses to the first and second contemplations.

After the preparatory prayer and the three preludes, it will be profitable, using the imagination, to apply the five senses to the first and second contemplations in the following manner:

The first point is to see the persons in my imagination, contemplating and meditating in detail the circumstances surrounding them, and I will then draw some spiritual profit from this scene.

The second point is to hear what they are saying, or what they might say, and I will reflect within myself to draw some fruit from what I have heard.

The third point is to smell and taste in my imagination the infinite fragrance and sweetness of the Divinity, and of the soul, and of its virtues, and of all else, according to the character of the person I am contemplating. And I will reflect within myself to draw spiritual profit therefrom.

The fourth point is to use in imagination the sense of touch, for example, by embracing and kissing the place where the persons walk or sit, always endeavoring to draw some spiritual fruit from this.

The colloquy. Conclude with a colloquy, and with the "Our Father," as in the first and second contemplations.

OBSERVATIONS

1. It is to be observed that during this week and the following weeks, I should read only the mystery concerned with the contemplation that I am on the point of making. Thus, for the time being, I should not read any mystery which I am not going to consider on that day or at that hour, so that the consideration of one mystery may not interfere with the consideration of another.

2. The first Exercise on the Incarnation will be made at midnight, the second at daybreak, the third at the hour of Mass, the fourth at the hour of Vespers, and the fifth before the supper hour. Each Exercise should continue for one hour, and the same order shall be observed in all that follows.

3. It should be noted that if the exercitant is old or weak, or even if he is robust, if he has been somewhat exhausted by the first week, it is better that in the second week, sometimes at least, he should not rise at midnight. He should then make one contemplation in the morning, another at the time of Mass, and another before dinner, with one repetition of these at the time of Vespers and the application of the five senses before supper.

4. In the second week, of all the ten additional directions mentioned for the first week, the second, sixth, and seventh, and part of the tenth, are to be changed.

The second direction will be to place before my mind, immediately on awaking, the subject of contemplation which I am going to make, desiring to know more thoroughly the eternal Word Incarnate, so that I may better serve and follow Him.

The sixth direction will be to call frequently to mind the life and the mysteries of Christ our Lord, from the Incarnation to the place of the mystery I am now contemplating.

The seventh direction will be that the exercitant should take care to make use of darkness or light, and of good or bad weather in so far as he feels that it can be useful in helping him to find what he desires.

The tenth direction will be that the exercitant must conduct himself according to the demands of the mysteries that he is contemplating, for some of them require penance and others do not. And so all ten additional directions are to be observed with great care.

5. In all the Exercises, except the one at midnight and the one in the morning, something equivalent to the second additional direction should be adopted in the following manner:

As soon as I remember that it is time for the Exercise which I am going to make, before entering into it, I will call to mind where I am going and into Whose presence. Then I will review briefly the Exercise I am about to make and, observing the third additional direction, I will begin the Exercise.

SECOND DAY

Take for the first and second contemplations, the Presentation in the Temple[1] and the Flight into Exile in Egypt.[2] Two repetitions should be made of these contemplations, and the application of the five senses, as was done the preceding day.

OBSERVATION

Even though the exercitant is strong and well disposed, sometimes it will be profitable to make some changes, from the second day to the fourth inclusive, in order that he may more readily find what he desires. Thus he may make only one contemplation at daybreak, and another about the time of Mass, and make a repetition of them at the time of Vespers, and the application of the senses before supper.

THIRD DAY

On this day use as subject matter how the Child Jesus was obedient to His parents at Nazareth,[3] and how afterwards

[1] P. 111.   [2] P. 111.   [3] P. 112.

they found Him in the temple.[4] Then make the two repetitions and the application of the senses.

PRELUDE TO THE CONSIDERATION OF THE STATES OF LIFE

We have already considered the example which Christ our Lord has given us for the first state of life, that is the observance of the commandments, in the meditation on His obedience to His parents. We have also considered the example that He gave us for the second state of life, that of evangelical perfection, when He remained in the temple, leaving His foster father and His Mother according to nature, that He might devote Himself entirely to the service of His heavenly Father. We will begin now to contemplate His life, and at the same time, to investigate and to ask in what kind of life or state His Divine Majesty wishes to make use of us.

Thus, as an introduction to this subject, in the first following Exercise we will consider the intention of Christ our Lord, and on the other hand that of the enemy of our human nature, and we will also consider how we ought to prepare ourselves to seek perfection in whatever state or kind of life that God our Lord shall grant us to choose.

FOURTH DAY

A MEDITATION ON TWO STANDARDS

The one of Christ our supreme Captain and Lord; the other of Lucifer, the mortal enemy of our human nature.

Prayer: The usual preparatory prayer.

The first prelude is the history of the subject matter. Here it will be how Christ our Lord calls and wants all men beneath His standard, and how Lucifer, on the contrary, wants all men under his.

The second prelude is the mental representation of the place. Here it will be to see a vast plain covering all the region

[4] P. 112.

about Jerusalem, where the supreme Leader of the good is Christ our Lord; and another plain in the region of Babylon, where the evil chieftain of the enemy is Lucifer.

The third prelude is to ask for what I desire. Here it will be to ask for a knowledge of the deceits of the evil chieftain and help to guard myself against them, and a knowledge of the true life which the supreme and true Leader reveals, and for the grace to imitate Him.

The first point is to imagine how the evil chieftain of all the enemy is seated in the center of the vast plain of Babylon, on a great throne of fire and smoke—a horrible and terrible sight to behold.

The second point is to consider how he calls together countless demons, and how he scatters them, some to one city, some to another, throughout the whole world, missing no province, no place, no state of life, nor even any single person.

The third point is to listen to the harangue which he delivers to them, how he spurs them on to ensnare men and to bind them in chains. He bids them first to tempt men with the lust of riches (as he is most accustomed to do), that they may thereby more easily gain the empty honor of the world, and then come to unbounded pride. The first step in his snare is that of riches, the second honor, and the third pride. From these three steps Satan leads on to all other vices.

In like manner, we are to imagine on the other hand, the supreme and true Leader, who is Christ our Lord.

The first point is to consider how Christ our Lord takes His stand in a lowly place, in that great plain about Jerusalem, and He is beautiful and gracious to behold.

The second point is to see how the Lord of the entire world chooses so many persons, apostles, disciples, etc., and sends them throughout the whole world to spread His sacred doctrine among men of every state and condition.

The third point is to listen to the discourse which Christ our Lord makes to all His servants and friends whom He sends on this mission, charging them that they should seek to help all men; first, by encouraging them to embrace the most perfect spiritual poverty, and if it should please His Divine Majesty, to choose them for it, also to embrace actual poverty. Secondly, by encouraging them to desire insults and contempt, for from these two things come humility. So then there are three steps: the first, poverty opposed to riches; the second, scorn or contempt, opposed to worldly honor; the third, humility, opposed to pride. From these three steps, let them lead men to all virtues.

Colloquy. I will now address a colloquy to our Lady and I will ask her to obtain for me from her Son and Lord the grace that I may be received under His standard, first, in the most perfect spiritual poverty, and should it so please His Divine Majesty to choose me, also in actual poverty; secondly in bearing reproaches and offenses, thus imitating Him more perfectly, provided only I can suffer them without sin on the part of any other person or displeasure to His Divine Majesty. Afterwards, I will say the "Hail Mary." I will ask the Son to obtain for me the same graces from the Father, and I will then recite the "Anima Christi."

I will also ask the Father to grant me the same graces, and I will say the "Our Father."

This Exercise will be made at midnight and again in the morning. There will also be two repetitions of the same Exercise at the time of Mass and at the time of Vespers, always ending with the three colloquys, with our Lady, with the Son, and with the Father. The meditation on the three classes of men, which follows, will be made an hour before supper.

THE THREE CLASSES OF MEN

On the same fourth day a meditation on the three classes of men is to be made, so that we may embrace that which is best.

Prayer: The usual preparatory prayer.

The first prelude is the history. Here it is to consider three classes of men. Each of them has acquired ten thousand ducats, but not purely, as they should have, for the love of God. These men all wish to save their souls and find peace in

God our Lord by freeing themselves of the serious impediment arising from their attachment to this acquired money.

The second prelude is the mental representation of the place. Here I will behold myself standing in the presence of God our Lord and all His saints, that I may desire and know what is most pleasing to His Divine Goodness.

The third prelude is to ask for what I desire. Here it will be to beg for the grace to choose what is for the greatest glory of His Divine Majesty and the salvation of my soul.

The first class. They would like to free themselves of the attachment they have for the money they acquired, in order to find peace in God our Lord, and to be able to save their souls, but up to the hour of death they do not take the means.

The second class. They want to free themselves of the attachment, but they wish to do so in such a way as to retain what they have acquired. They thus want God to come to what they desire, and they do not resolve to give up the money in order to go to God, even though this would be the better state for them.

The third class. They wish to free themselves of the attachment, but in such a way that their inclination will be neither to retain the thing acquired nor not to retain it, desiring to act only as God our Lord shall inspire them and as it shall seem better to them for the service and praise of His Divine Majesty. Meanwhile they wish to consider that they have in their hearts broken all the attachments, striving not to desire that thing nor anything else, unless it be only the service of God our Lord that prompts their action. Thus, the desire of being able to serve God our Lord better will move them either to accept things or to give them up.

Colloquy. Make the same three colloquies that were made in the previous contemplation or the two standards.

NOTE

It is to be noted that when we feel an attachment opposed to actual poverty or a repugnance to it, when we are not indifferent to poverty or riches, it is of great help in overcoming this inordinate attachment to beg in the *colloquies* (even though our flesh opposes it), that our Lord choose to have us serve Him in actual poverty, and that we desire it, beg for it and plead for it, provided that it be only for the service and praise of His Divine Goodness.

FIFTH DAY

The contemplation is on the departure of Christ our Lord from Nazareth to the River Jordan, and how He was baptized.[5]

Notes

This contemplation will be made at midnight and again in the morning. Two repetitions will be made at the time of Mass and at the hour of Vespers. Before supper the application of the senses to the mystery will be made.

Each of these five Exercises will be preceded by the usual preparatory prayer, then the three preludes, as was fully explained in the contemplations on the Incarnation and the Nativity.[6] The Exercise will end with the three colloquies of the contemplation of the three classes of men, or according to the note that follows that Exercise.[7]

The particular examination of conscience after the noon meal and after supper will be made on the faults and negligences relating to the Exercises of the day and to the additional directions. This same procedure will be observed on the following days.

SIXTH DAY

Contemplation on how Christ our Lord went from the River Jordan to the desert and the events that took place at this time.[8]

The same procedure will be observed as on the fifth day.

[5] P. 113.
[6] P. 73.
[7] P. 78.
[8] P. 113.

SEVENTH DAY

How St. Andrew and the others followed Christ our Lord.[9]

EIGHTH DAY

The Sermon on the Mount, which is on the Eight Beatitudes.[10]

NINTH DAY

How Christ appeared to His disciples on the waves of the sea.[11]

TENTH DAY

How our Lord preached in the temple.[12]

ELEVENTH DAY

The resurrection of Lazarus.[13]

TWELFTH DAY

Palm Sunday.[14]

[9] P. 113.
[10] P. 114.
[11] P. 115.
[12] P. 118.
[13] P. 117.
[14] P. 118.

NOTES

1. The number of contemplations of this second week may be extended or diminished depending on the time which each one wishes to spend or according to the progress he is making. If he wishes to increase them, he may take the mysteries of the visitation of our Lady to St. Elizabeth,[15] the shepherds, the Circumcision of the Child Jesus,[16] the Three Kings,[17] and also others. If he wishes to shorten them, he may omit some of the mysteries mentioned above. These are meant to serve as an introduction and method for better and more complete contemplation later.

2. The discussion of the choice of a way of life shall begin with the contemplation on the departure of our Lord from Nazareth for the River Jordan and the events included therein,[18] as explained later in the contemplation on the fifth day.

3. Before entering upon this choice of a way of life, and in order to inspire within ourselves a love for the true doctrine of Christ our Lord, it is very helpful to make the following meditation on the three forms of humility, and to reflect upon them from time to time throughout the day. We should likewise make the colloquies that will be mentioned further on.

THE THREE MODES OF HUMILITY

The first mode of humility is necessary for eternal salvation. This requires that I humble and abase myself as much as is possible for me, in order that I may obey in all things the law of God our Lord. Accordingly I would not give consideration to the thought of breaking any commandment, divine or human, that binds me under pain of mortal sin, even

15 P. 109.
16 P. 110.
17 P. 111.
18 P. 113.

though this offense would make me master of all creation or would preserve my life on earth.

The second mode of humility is more perfect than the first. I am in possession of it if my state of mind is such that I neither desire nor even prefer to have riches rather than poverty, to seek honor rather than dishonor, to have a long life rather than a short one, provided that here be the same opportunity to serve God our Lord, and to save my soul. Nor would I, for the sake of all creation or for the purpose of saving my life, consider committing a single venial sin.

The third mode of humility is the most perfect. This exists when, the first and second forms already possessed and the praise and glory of the Divine Majesty being equally served, I desire and choose poverty with Christ poor rather than riches, in order to be more like Christ our Lord. When I choose reproaches with Christ thus suffering rather than honor, and when I am willing to be considered as worthless and a fool for Christ Who suffered such treatment before me, rather than to be esteemed as wise and prudent in this world.

If one desires to attain this third form of humility it will be very profitable for him to make the three colloquies on the three classes of men mentioned above.[19] He should implore our Lord to be pleased to choose him for this third form of humility, which is greater and more perfect, so that he may better imitate and serve Him, provided it be for the equal or greater service and praise of His Divine Majesty.

INTRODUCTION TO MAKING A CHOICE OF A WAY OF LIFE

In every good choice, in so far as it depends upon us, the direction of our intention should be simple. I must look only to the end for which I am created, that is, for the praise of God our Lord and for the salvation of my soul. Therefore, whatever I choose must have as its purpose to help me to

[19] P. 78.

this end. I must not shape or draw the end to the means, but the means to the end. Many, for example, first choose marriage, which is a means, and secondarily to serve God our Lord in the married state, which service of God is the end. Likewise there are others who first desire to have benefices, and afterward to serve God in them. These individuals do not go straight to God, but want God to come straight to their inordinate attachments. Acting thus, they make a means of the end, and an end of the means, so that what they ought to seek first, they seek last. My first aim, then, should be my desire to serve God, which is the end, and after this, to seek a benefice or to marry, if it is more fitting for me, for these things are but means to the end. Thus, nothing should move me to use such means or to deprive myself of them except it be only the service and praise of God our Lord and the eternal salvation of my soul.

A CONSIDERATION TO OBTAIN INFORMATION ON THE MATTERS IN WHICH A CHOICE SHOULD BE MADE

This contains four points and a note:

First point: All matters in which we wish to make a choice must be either indifferent or good in themselves. They must meet with the approbation of our Holy Mother, the hierarchical Church, and not be bad or repugnant to her.

Second point: There are some things that are the objects of an immutable choice, such as the priesthood, matrimony, etc. There are others in which the choice is not immutable, as for example, accepting or relinquishing a benefice, accepting or renouncing temporal goods.

Third point: Once an immutable choice has been made there is no further choice, for it cannot be dissolved, as is true with marriage, the priesthood, etc. It should be noted only that if one has not made this choice properly, with due consideration, and without inordinate attachments, he should repent and try to lead a good life in the choice that he has made. Since this choice was ill considered and improperly made, it does not seem to be a vocation from God, as many err in believing, wishing to interpret an ill-considered or bad choice as a divine call. For every divine call is always pure and clean without any admixture of flesh or other inordinate attachments.

Fourth point: If one has made a proper and well-considered choice that is mutable, and has not been influenced either by the flesh or the world, there is no reason why he should make a new choice. But he should perfect himself as much as possible in the choice he has made.

Note

It is to be noted that if this mutable choice is not well considered and sincerely made, then it will be profitable to make the choice anew in the proper manner. If one wishes to bring forth fruits that are worthwhile and pleasing to God our Lord.

THREE OCCASIONS WHEN A WISE AND GOOD CHOICE CAN BE MADE

The first occasion is when God our Lord moves and attracts the will so that the devout soul, without question and without desire to question, follows what has been manifested to it. St. Paul and St. Matthew did this when they followed Christ our Lord.

The second occasion is present when one has developed a clear understanding and knowledge through the experience of consolations and desolations and the discernment of diverse spirits.

The third occasion is in a time of tranquillity. Here one considers first for what purpose man is born, which is to praise God our Lord and to save his soul. Since he desires to attain this end, he chooses some life or state within the bounds of the church that will help him in the service of God our Lord and the salvation of his soul. I said "a time of tranquility," when the soul is not agitated by diverse spirits, and is freely and calmly making use of its natural powers.

IF A CHOICE HAS NOT BEEN MADE ON THE FIRST OR SECOND OCCASION, BELOW ARE GIVEN TWO METHODS OF MAKING IT DURING THE THIRD OCCASION

The first method of making a wise and good choice contains six points:

The first point: To place before my mind's eye the thing on which I wish to make a choice. It may be an office or a benefice to be accepted or refused, or anything else that is the object of a mutable choice.

The second point: I must have as my aim the end for which I am created, which is the praise of God our Lord and the salvation of my soul. At the same time I must remain indifferent and free from any inordinate attachments so that I am not more inclined or disposed to take the thing proposed than to reject it, nor to relinquish it rather than to accept it. I must rather be like the equalized scales of balance, ready to follow the course which I feel is more for the glory and praise of God our Lord and the salvation of my soul.

The third point: I must ask God our Lord to deign to move my will and to reveal to my spirit what I should do to best promote His praise and glory in the matter of choice. After examining the matter thoroughly and faithfully with my understanding, I should make my choice in conformity with His good pleasure and His most holy will.

The fourth point: I will use my reason to weigh the many advantages and benefits that would accrue to me if I held the proposed office or benefice solely for the praise of God our Lord and the salvation of my soul. I will likewise consider and weigh the disadvantages and dangers that there are in holding it. I will proceed in like manner with the other alternative, that is, examine and consider the advantages and benefits as well as the disadvantages and dangers in not holding the proposed office or benefice.

The fifth point: After having thus weighed the matter and carefully examined it from every side, I will consider which alternative appears more reasonable. Acting upon the stronger judgment of reason and not on any inclination of the senses, I must come to a decision in the matter that I am considering.

The sixth point: After such a choice or decision has been reached I should turn with great diligence to prayer in the presence of God our Lord and offer Him this choice that His Divine Majesty may deign to accept and confirm it, if it be to His greater service and praise.

The second method of making a wise and good choice contains four rules and a note:

The first rule is that the love which moves me and causes me to make this choice should come from above, that is from the love of God, so that before I make my choice I will feel that the greater or lesser love that I have for the thing chosen is solely for the sake of my Creator and Lord.

The second rule is to consider some man that I have never seen or known, and in whom I wish to see complete perfection. Now I should consider what I would tell him to do and choose for the greater glory of God our Lord and the greater perfection of his soul. I will act in like manner myself, keeping the rule that I have proposed for another.

The third rule is to consider that if I were at the point of death, what form and procedure I would wish to have observed in making this present choice. Guiding myself by this consideration, I will make my decision on the whole matter.

The fourth rule is to examine and consider how I shall be on the day of judgment, to think how I shall then wish to have made my decision in the present matter. The rule which I should then wish to have followed, I will now follow, that I may on that day be filled with joy and delight.

NOTE

Taking the above mentioned rules as my guide for eternal salvation and peace, I will make my choice and offer myself to God our Lord, following the sixth point of the first method of making a choice.

DIRECTIONS FOR AMENDING AND REFORMING ONE'S LIFE AND STATE

It is to be observed that those who hold ecclesiastical office or who are married (whether they are rich in worldly possessions or not), when they do not have an opportunity to make a decision or are not very willing to do so regarding things that are subject to choice, that instead of having them make a choice it is very profitable to give to each a form and method of amending and reforming his own life and state. This may be done by placing before him the purpose of his creation, life and state, which is the glory and praise of God our Lord and the salvation of his own soul.

If he wishes to attain and fulfill this end he should consider and examine thoroughly, using the Exercises and the methods of making a choice, explained above, how large a house and establishment he should maintain; how he should manage and govern it; how he should guide it by word and example. He ought also to consider what portion of his means he should use for his family and household, and how much should be given to the poor and to other pious works. In all these works he should desire and seek nothing but the greatest praise and glory of God our Lord. For each one must realize that he will make progress in all spiritual matters in proportion to his flight from self-love, self-will, and self-interest.

THIRD WEEK

FIRST DAY AND FIRST CONTEMPLATION

The first contemplation at midnight is how Christ our Lord went from Bethany to Jerusalem, including the Last Supper.[1] It contains the preparatory prayer, three preludes, six points, and a colloquy.

Prayer: The usual preparatory prayer.

The first prelude is to call to mind the history, which is here how Christ our Lord, while at Bethany, sent two disciples to Jerusalem to prepare the supper, and afterwards He Himself went there with the other disciples. How after they had eaten the Pascal Lamb and supped, He washed their feet and gave His Most Holy Body and His Most Precious Blood to His disciples. How He gave His last discourse after Judas had gone to sell his Lord.

The second prelude is a mental representation of the place. Here it will be to consider the road from Bethany to Jerusalem, whether it is broad or narrow, whether it is level, etc. Consider likewise the room of the supper; whether it is large or small, its general appearance.

The third prelude is to ask for what I desire. Here it will be to ask for sorrow, affliction, and confusion because the Lord is going to His passion on account of my sins.

The first point is to visualize the persons at the supper, and reflecting within myself, to strive to gain some profit from them.

The second point is to listen to what they say, and likewise to draw some profit from it.

The third point is to observe what they are doing and to draw some fruit from it.

The fourth point is to consider what Christ our Lord suffers in His humanity or wills to suffer, according to the passage that is being contemplated. Here I will begin with

[1] P. 118.

serious effort to strive to grieve, to be sad, and lament. I will strive in like manner through the following points.

The fifth point is to consider how the Divinity hides Itself. That is to say, how It could destroy Its enemies and does not do so, how It leaves the most Sacred Humanity to suffer so cruelly.

The sixth point is to consider that all of the suffering is for my sins, and what I ought to do and suffer for Him.

Colloquy. Conclude with a colloquy to Christ our Lord, and at the end say the "Our Father."

NOTE

It is to be observed, as has already been stated in part, that in the colloquies I must exercise my reason and make supplication according to the present circumstances. That is to say, whether I am being tempted or experiencing consolation, whether I wish to have one virtue or another, whether I am trying to dispose myself in one direction or another, whether I desire to lament or rejoice in the matter of my contemplation. Finally, I shall ask for what I most earnestly desire regarding the particular things that I am considering. In this way I may have just one colloquy with Christ our Lord, or if the subject matter or devotion prompts me to do so, I may make three colloquies, one with the Blessed Mother, one with the Son, and one with the Father, in the manner that was prescribed in the second week, in the meditation on two standards,[2] together with the note following the meditation on the three classes of men.[3]

SECOND CONTEMPLATION

The second contemplation in the morning will be on the mysteries from the Last Supper to the Garden inclusive.[4]

Prayer: The usual preparatory prayer.

The first prelude is the history. Here it will be how Christ

2 P. 76.
3 P. 78.
4 P. 119.

our Lord descended with his eleven disciples from Mount Sion, where the Supper was held, to the Valley of Josaphat. Leaving the eight in one part of the valley, He took the other three apart into the Garden. He then began to pray and His sweat became drops of blood. Three times He prayed to His Father, and three times he aroused His disciples from sleep. After His enemies fell to the ground at the sound of His voice, and Judas gave him the kiss of peace, after He restored the ear of Malchus which Peter had cut off, He was seized like a malefactor and He was led through the valley and back up the slope to the house of Annas.

The second prelude is a visualization of the place. Here it will be to consider the road from Mount Sion to the Valley of Josaphat, and likewise the Garden; its width, its length, and its general appearance.

The third prelude is to ask for what I desire. In the Passion the proper thing to ask for is grief with Christ suffering, a broken heart with Christ heartbroken, tears, and deep suffering because of the great suffering that Christ endured for me.

NOTES

1. In this second contemplation, after the preparatory prayer and the three preludes already mentioned, the same procedure is to be followed for the points and colloquies as is found in the first contemplation on the Last Supper. At the hour of Mass and at Vespers time, two repetitions will be made on the first and second contemplations. Then, before supper, the application of the senses will be made on the matter of these two contemplations, always beginning with the preparatory prayer and the three preludes, according to the subject matter. The form is the same as that prescribed and explained for the second week.

2. As far as age, temperament, and disposition permit, the exercitant will make each day the five Exercises, or fewer.

3. In the third week the second and sixth additional directions may be modified in part. The second direction shall now be to consider as soon as I awake, where I am going

and to what purpose. I shall make a short review of the contemplation that I wish to make. Depending on the subject matter of the mystery, I will strive while rising and dressing to arouse sentiments of sorrow and grief within myself because of the great sorrow and suffering of Christ our Lord.

The sixth additional direction will now be that I will strive not to permit myself any joyful thoughts, even though they are good and holy, as are those of the Resurrection and the glory of heaven. I will rather rouse myself to sorrow, suffering, and deep pain, frequently calling to mind the labors, burdens, and suffering that Christ our Lord bore from the moment of His birth up to the mystery of His Passion, which I am now contemplating.

4. The particular examination of conscience on the Exercises and the additional directions as given for this week, will be made in the same way as in the past week.

SECOND DAY

On the second day the contemplation at midnight will be on the events from the Garden to the house of Annas inclusive.[5] In the morning the contemplation will be on the events from the house of Annas to the house of Caiphas inclusive.[6] Then there will be the two repetitions and the application of the senses, as already stated.

THIRD DAY

The contemplation at midnight will be on the events from the house of Caiphas to that of Pilate inclusive.[7] In the morn-Herod inclusive.[8] Then the repetitions and the application of the senses, as above.

[5] P. 119.
[6] P. 120.
[7] P. 120.
[8] P. 121.

FOURTH DAY

At midnight the subject matter will be from Herod to Pilate.[9] This contemplation will be on the first half of what took place in the house of Pilate. The morning contemplation will be on the remaining part. Then there will be the two repetitions and the application of the senses, as stated.

FIFTH DAY

At midnight, from the house of Pilate to the nailing to the cross,[10] and in the morning, from the raising of the cross to His death.[11] Then the repetitions and the application of the senses.

SIXTH DAY

At midnight from the taking down from the cross to the burial in the sepulcher exclusive,[12] and in the morning, from the burial in the sepulcher inclusive to the house where our Lady was after the burial of her Son.

SEVENTH DAY

A contemplation of the entire Passion in the exercise of midnight and in the morning.

Instead of the two repetitions and the application of the senses, consider as frequently as possible throughout the entire day how the most Sacred Body of Christ our Lord re-

[9] P. 121.
[10] P. 121.
[11] P. 122.
[12] P. 122.

mained separated and apart from His Soul, also where and how it was buried. Consider likewise the desolation of our Lady, her great grief and weariness, also that of the disciples.

NOTE

It is to be observed that anyone who wishes to spend more time on the Passion may consider fewer mysteries in each contemplation, for example, in the first contemplation, on the Last Supper; in the second, the washing of feet; in the third, the institution of the Blessed Sacrament; in the fourth, our Lord's last discourse, and so on for the other contemplations and mysteries.

In like manner, after the Passion has been completed, one may give an entire day to meditation on the first half of the Passion, a second day to the other half, and a third day to the entire Passion. On the other hand, anyone wishing to spend a shorter time on the Passion, may take at midnight the Last Supper and the Garden; in the morning at the time of Mass, the house of Annas; at Vespers, the house of Caiphas; in place of the Exercise of the time before supper, the house of Pilate. Thus omitting the repetitions and the application of the senses, he may make five distinct Exercises each day, and in each Exercise contemplate a distinct mystery of the Passion of Christ our Lord.

After he has thus completed the Passion, he may use another day to contemplate the entire Passion in one Exercise, or in several, in the way that he thinks will profit him most.

RULES TO BE OBSERVED IN THE FUTURE IN THE MATTER OF FOOD

1. There is less need to abstain from bread for it is not the kind of food over which the appetite is usually inclined to be uncontrolled, or over which temptation is so insistent as with other kinds.

2. Abstinence is more appropriate with regard to drink than to eating bread. Therefore one must consider care-

fully what would be beneficial to him and therefore permissible, and also what would be harmful, and so to be avoided.

3. With regard to foods, greater and more complete abstinence must be practiced because here temptation is likely to be more insistent and the appetite inclined to be excessive. In order to avoid overindulgence, abstinence may be observed in two ways: by accustoming oneself to eat coarse foods, or if delicacies are taken, to eat them sparingly.

4. While taking care not to become sick, the more one abstains in the quantity of food suited to him, the sooner he will arrive at the mean he should observe in eating and drinking. There are two reasons for this: first, by thus helping and disposing himself he will more frequently feel the interior directions, consolations, and divine inspirations that will show him the mean that is proper for him. Secondly, if he finds that with such abstinence he lacks sufficient health and strength for the Spiritual Exercises, he will easily be able to judge what is more suitable for sustaining his body.

5. While one is eating, he may consider that he sees Christ our Lord at table with His Apostles, how He eats and drinks; how He looks and how He speaks, and he will strive to imitate Him. He will thus keep his understanding occupied principally with our Lord, and less with the sustenance of his own body. Thus he may adopt a better method and order in the manner in which he should govern himself.

6. While eating, he may at other times consider the lives of the saints or some other pious contemplation, or he may consider some spiritual work that he has to perform. If he is occupied with such matters, he will take less delight and sensual pleasure in the nourishment of his body.

7. Above all, he must take care that his mind is not entirely occupied in what he is eating, and that he is not carried away by his appetite into eating hurriedly. Let him rather master himself both in the way that he eats and the amount that he takes.

8. To avoid excess, it is very useful after dinner or after supper, or at another time when one feels no desire to eat, to make a determination for the next dinner or supper,

and so for the subsequent days, on the amount of food that is proper for him to eat. Let him not exceed this amount, no matter how strong his appetite or the temptation. Rather, the better to overcome every disorderly appetite and temptation of the enemy, if he is tempted to eat more, he should eat less.

FOURTH WEEK

FIRST CONTEMPLATION

How Christ our Lord appeared to our Lady
Prayer: The usual preparatory prayer.

The first prelude is the history. Here it is how after Christ expired on the cross, and His body remained separated from the soul, yet always united with the Divinity. His soul likewise united with the Divinity, descended into hell. There He released the souls of the just, then returning to the sepulcher, and rising again, he appeared in body and soul to His Blessed Mother.

The second prelude is the mental examination of the place. Here it will be to see the arrangement of the holy sepulcher and the place or house of our Lady, noting its different rooms; likewise her room, her oratory, etc.

The third prelude is to ask for what I desire. Here it will be to request the grace that I may feel intense joy and gladness for the great glory and joy of Christ our Lord.

The first, second, and third points are the same that we have had in the contemplation on the Last Supper of Chirst our Lord.

The fourth point is to consider that the Divinity which seemed to hide itself during the Passion, now appears and manifests itself so miraculously in the most holy Resurrection by its true and most holy effects.

The fifth point is to consider the office of consoler that Christ our Lord exercises, comparing it with the way that friends are wont to console one another.

Colloquy. Conclude with one or more colloquies according to the subject matter and then with the "Our Father."

Note

1. In the following contemplations all of the mysteries from the Resurrection to the Ascension inclusive are to be

made in the manner indicated below, observing in other respects throughout the Week of the Resurrection the same form and methods that are followed during the entire Week of the Passion.

The exercitant may use this first contemplation on the Resurrection as a guide. The preludes will be the same, adapted to the subject matter, and the five points will be the same. The additional directions will be the same, with the changes given below. In all the rest, that is, the repetitions, the application of the senses, the shortening or lengthening of the mysteries, the Week of the Passion may serve as a guide.

2. Ordinarily, it is more suitable in the fourth week than in the other three, to make four Exercises instead of five. The first on rising in the morning; the second at the hour of Mass or before dinner, in place of the first repetition; the third at the hour of Vespers, in place of the second repetition; the fourth before supper, will be the application of the senses to the three Exercises of the day.

In this Exercise more attention and time is to be given to the principal points and to those parts in which greater spiritual satisfaction and fruit are experienced.

3. Although in all contemplations a definite number of points is given, that is, three or five, etc., the one making the contemplation may use more or fewer points, as seems better to him. For this reason it is very useful, before beginning the contemplation, to foresee and determine the number of points that he is to use.

4. In this fourth week, the second, sixth, seventh and tenth additional directions are to be changed.

The second will be that upon waking, I will see in my mind's eye the contemplation that I am about to make and I will strive to feel joy and gladness at the great joy and gladness of Christ our Lord. The sixth will be to occupy my mind and thoughts with things that cause pleasure, happiness, and spiritual joy, for example, the thought of heaven.

The seventh will be to take advantage of the light and the comforts of the season, for example, the refreshing breezes of spring and summer, and the warmth of the sun and of a fire in winter, in so far as the soul thinks or can presume that these things may help it to rejoice in its Creator and Redeemer.

The tenth will be, in place of penance, to concentrate on obtaining temperance and moderation in all things, except when fasting and abstinence are required by the Church, for these prescriptions must always be observed unless there is some legitimate impediment to their fulfillment.

CONTEMPLATION TO ATTAIN DIVINE LOVE

Two points are to be noted here:

The first is that love ought to be manifested in deeds rather than words.

The second is that love consists in a mutual interchange by the two parties, that is to say, that the lover give to and share with the beloved all that he has or can attain, and that the beloved act toward the lover in like manner. Thus if he has knowledge, he shares it with the one who does not have it. In like manner they share honors, riches, and all things.

Prayer: The usual preparatory prayer.

The first prelude is the mental representation of the place. Here it is to see how I stand in the presence of God our Lord and of the angels and saints, who intercede for me.

The second prelude is to ask for what I desire. Here it will be to ask for a deep knowledge of the many blessings I have received, that I may be filled with gratitude for them, and in all things love and serve the Divine Majesty.

The first point is to call to mind the benefits that I have received from creation, redemption, and the particular gifts I have received. I will ponder with great affection how much God our Lord has done for me, and how many of His graces He has given me. I will likewise consider how much the same Lord wishes to give Himself to me in so far as He can, according to His divine decrees. I will then reflect within myself, and consider that I, for my part, with great reason and justice, should offer and give to His Divine Majesty, all that I possess and myself with it, as one who makes an offering with deep affection, saying:

Take, O Lord, and receive all my liberty, my memory, my understanding, and my entire will, all that I have and possess. Thou hast given all to me, to Thee O Lord, I return it. All is Thine; dispose of it according to Thy will. Give me Thy love and Thy grace, for this is enough for me.

The second point is to consider how God dwells in His creatures: in the elements, giving them being; in the plants, giving them life; in the animals, giving them sensation; in men, giving them understanding. So He dwells in me, giving me being, life, sensation, and intelligence, and making a temple of me, since He created me to the likeness and image of His Divine Majesty. Then I will reflect upon myself in the manner stated in the first point, or in any other way that may seem more beneficial.

The same procedure should be observed in each of the points that follow.

The third point is to consider how God works and labors for me in all created things on the face of the earth, that is, He conducts Himself as one who labors; in the heavens, the elements, plants, fruits, flocks, etc. He gives them being, preserves them, grants them growth, sensation, etc. Then I will reflect on myself.

The fourth point is to consider how all blessings and gifts descend from above. My limited power, for example, comes from the supreme and infinite power from above. In like manner justice, goodness, pity, mercy, etc., descend from above just as the rays from the sun, the waters from the spring, etc. Then I will reflect upon myself, as explained above, and conclude with a colloquy and the "Our Father."

THREE METHODS OF PRAYER

THE FIRST METHOD OF PRAYER

The first method of prayer is on the Ten Commandments, the seven capital sins, the three powers of the soul, and the five senses of the body. The purpose of this method of prayer is to provide a method of procedure, and some exercises in which the soul may prepare itself and make progress, thereby making its prayer more acceptable, rather than to give a form and method of praying.

Additional direction. Some exercise equivalent to the second additional direction of the second week[1] is to be made. Thus, before entering on prayer, I will let my mind repose a little, and sitting or walking, according as shall seem best to me, I will consider where I am going, and for what purpose. This addition will be made at the beginning of all the methods of prayer.

Prayer: Then a preparatory prayer is to be made, such as to ask of God our Lord the grace to know how I have failed in regard to the Ten Commandments. I should likewise ask for grace and help to amend myself in the future, asking for a perfect understanding of the commandments so that I may observe them better, to the greater praise and glory of His Divine Majesty.

I. *The Ten Commandments*

Method: For the first method of prayer, it is well to consider and to think over the first commandment, how I have kept it, and in which I have failed. For this consideration, I will take, as a rule, the time required to recite three times the "Our Father" and the "Hail Mary." If in this time I discover faults I have committed, I will ask pardon and forgiveness for them, and say an "Our Father." I will follow this same method for each of the Ten Commandments.

[1] P. 73.

Note: It is to be observed that when one comes to a commandment against which he is not in the habit of sinning, it is not necessary to delay so long on it, but according as he realizes that he offends more or less in a commandment, he should spend a greater or lesser time in its consideration and examination.

The same procedure should be observed regarding the capital sins.

After I have completed this form of consideration on all the commandments, accused myself where I have failed, and asked for grace and help to amend my life in the future, I will conclude with a colloquy to God our Lord, according to the subject matter.

II. *The Capital Sins*

Method: Regarding the seven capital sins, after the additional direction, the preparatory prayer is to be made in the manner already prescribed, the only change is that the matter here is the sins which are to be avoided, whereas before it was the commandments to be observed. In like manner the procedure and the rule prescribed above are to be observed, together with the colloquy.

In order to know better the faults committed relating to the capital sins, let the contrary virtues be considered. Thus the better to avoid these sins, one should resolve and endeavor by devout exercises to acquire and retain the seven virtues contrary to them.

III. *The Powers of the Soul*

Method: The same method and rule that were followed for the commandments should be observed with regard to the three powers of the soul, with the addition, preparatory prayer, and colloquy.

IV. *The Five Senses of the Body*

Method: The same method will also be followed with regard to the five senses of the body, only the subject matter is changed.

Note: Whoever wishes to imitate Christ our Lord in the use of the senses should recommend himself to His Divine Majesty in the preparatory prayer, and after the consideration of each of the senses say a "Hail Mary" or an "Our Father." If he wishes to imitate our Lady in the use of the senses, he should recommend himself to her in the preparatory prayer, that she may obtain this grace for him from her Son and Lord. After the consideration of each sense, he should say a "Hail Mary."

THE SECOND METHOD OF PRAYER

The second method consists in contemplating the meaning of each word of a prayer.

Additional direction: The same additional direction that was made in the first method of prayer will also be used here.

The preparatory prayer will be made according to the person to whom the prayer is directed.

The second method of prayer is as follows: The person may be kneeling or sitting, whichever suits his disposition better and is more conducive to devotion. He should keep his eyes closed, or fixed on one position, not permitting them to wander about. He should then say, "Father," and reflect upon this word as long as he finds meanings, comparisons, relish, and consolation in the consideration of it. He should then continue the same method with each word of the "Our Father," or of any other prayer that he may wish to contemplate in this manner.

Rules

I. He will continue in the prescribed manner for one hour on the "Our Father." When this prayer is finished, he will say the "Hail Mary," the "Creed," the *"Anima Christi"* and the "Hail Holy Queen," vocally or mentally, in the customary manner.

II. During the contemplation on the "Our Father," if he finds in one or two words good matter for thought, relish, and consolation, he should not be anxious to pass on, even though he spend the entire hour on what he has found. When the hour is over, he will say the rest of the "Our Father" in the usual way.

III. If he has spent the entire hour dwelling on one or two words of the "Our Father," on another day, when he wishes to return to the same prayer, he may say the above-mentioned word or two in the usual way, and begin the contemplation of the word which immediately follows, as explained in the second rule.

Note I. When he has finished the "Our Father," after one or more days, he should contemplate the "Hail Mary" in the same manner, and then the other prayers, so that for some time he is always occupied with one of them.

Note II. When the prayer is finished, he should turn to the Person to whom the prayer is directed, and ask for the virtues and graces which he feels the greatest need.

THE THIRD METHOD OF PRAYER

The third method of prayer is a rhythmical recitation.

The additional direction is the same as in the first and second methods of prayer.

The third method of prayer is that, at each breath or respiration, he is to pray mentally, as he says one word of the "Our Father," or any other prayer that is being recited, so that between one breath and another a single word is said. During this same space of time, he is to give his full attention to the meaning of the word, or to the person whom he is addressing, or to his own unworthiness, or to the difference between the greatness of this Person and his own lowliness. He will continue, observing the same procedure and rule, through the other words of the "Our Father" and the other prayers, namely, the "Hail Mary," the *"Anima Christi,"* the "Creed" and the "Hail Holy Queen."

Rule I. On another day, or at another hour, when he wishes to pray, he may say the "Hail Mary" in this rhythmical measure, and the other prayers in the usual way. He may then proceed to the other prayers in the same manner.

Rule II. If he wishes to spend a longer time in this measured prayer, he may say all of the above-mentioned prayers, or some of them, observing the same method of rhythmical breathing described above.

THE MYSTERIES OF THE LIFE OF OUR LORD

It will be noted that in all of the following mysteries the words in parentheses are taken from the Gospel itself but not the other words.[1] Three points are usually given for each mystery, to facilitate the contemplation and meditation.

THE ANNUNCIATION OF OUR LADY
(*Luke 1: 26–38*), p. 145

First Point—The Angel, St. Gabriel, greeted our Lady and announced to her the conception of Christ our Lord. *And when the Angel had come to her, he said: "Hail, full of grace. . . . Thou shalt conceive in thy womb and shalt bring forth a son."*

Second Point—The Angel confirms what he had said to our Lady by announcing the conception of St. John the Baptist, saying to her: *"And behold, Elizabeth thy kinswoman also has conceived a son in her old age."*

Third Point—Our Lady replied to the Angel: *"Behold the handmaid of the Lord; be it done to me according to thy word."*

THE VISITATION OF OUR LADY TO ELIZABETH
(*Luke 1: 39–56*), p. 146

First Point—When our Lady visited St. Elizabeth, St. John the Baptist, in his mother's womb, felt the visitation

---

[1] The parentheses of the *Autograph* have been replaced here with italics. It will be noted that in most instances St. Ignatius selected key phrases rather than citing complete verses from the Gospel. The same procedure has been followed in the translation; the text used is that of the Confraternity edition. The complete text suggested by Ignatius and given beneath the title of each meditation will be found in the appendix at the given page reference.

made by our Lady. When Elizabeth heard the greeting of Mary, the babe in her womb leapt. And Elizabeth was filled with the Holy Spirit, and cried out with a loud voice, saying, "Blessed art thou among women and blessed is the fruit of thy womb!"

Second Point – Our Lady chants the canticle, saying: "My soul magnifies the Lord."

Third Point – And Mary remained with her about three months and returned to her own house.

THE BIRTH OF CHRIST OUR LORD
(Luke 2: 1–14), p. 147

First Point – Our Lady and her spouse, St. Joseph, go from Nazareth to Bethlehem. And Joseph also went up from Galilee to Bethlehem, in obedience to Caesar, with Mary his espoused wife who was with child.

Second Point – And she brought forth her firstborn son, and wrapped him in swaddling clothes, and laid him in a manger.

Third Point – And suddenly there was a multitude of the heavenly host praising God and saying: "Glory to God in the highest."

THE SHEPHERDS
(Luke 2: 8–20), p. 148

First Point – The birth of Christ our Lord is made known to the shepherds by an angel: "I bring you good news of great joy, for today a Savior has been born to you."

Second Point – The shepherds go to Bethlehem. So they went with haste, and they found Mary and Joseph, and the babe lying in the manger.

Third Point – And the shepherds returned glorifying and praising God.

THE CIRCUMCISION
(Luke 2: 21), p. 149

First Point – They circumcised the Child Jesus.

Second Point – His name was called Jesus, the name given him by the angel before he was conceived in the womb.

Third Point – They return the Child to His mother, who felt compassion at the blood shed by her Son.

THE THREE MAGI KINGS
(*Matt.* 2: 1–12), p. 149

First Point – The three Magi Kings, guided by the star, came to adore Jesus, saying: "*We have seen his star in the East and have come to worship him.*"

Second Point – They adored Him and offered Him gifts. "*And falling down they worshipped him, and offered him gifts of gold, frankincense and myrrh.*

Third Point – *And being warned in a dream not to return to Herod, they went back to their own country by another way.*

THE PURIFICATION OF OUR LADY AND THE PRESENTATION OF THE CHILD JESUS
(*Luke* 2: 22–39), p. 150

First Point – They take the Child Jesus to the Temple to be presented to the Lord as the firstborn, and they offer for Him *a pair of turtle doves and two young pigeons.*

Second Point – Simeon, coming into the Temple, *also received him into his arms, saying: "Now thou dost dismiss thy servant, O Lord, according to thy word, in peace."*

Third Point – Anna, *coming up at that very hour, began to give praise to the Lord, and spoke of him to all who were awaiting the redemption of Jerusalem.*

THE FLIGHT INTO EGYPT
(*Matt.* 2: 13–15), p. 151

First Point – Herod wanted to kill the Child Jesus, and so he slew the Innocents. Before their slaughter an angel warned Joseph to fly into Egypt: "*Arise and take the child and his mother and flee into Egypt.*"

Second Point – He set out for Egypt. *So he arose, and took*

the child and his mother by night, and withdrew into Egypt.
Third Point – There he remained until the death of Herod.

THE RETURN FROM EGYPT
(*Matt.* 2: 19–23), p. 151

First Point – The angel admonishes Joseph to return to Israel: "*Arise, and take the child and his mother and go into the land of Israel.*"
Second Point – *So he arose . . . and went into the land of Israel.*
Third Point – *Since Archelaus, the son of Herod, ruled in Judea, he withdrew to Nazareth.*

THE LIFE OF OUR LORD FROM THE AGE OF TWELVE TO THE AGE OF THIRTY
(*Luke* 2: 51–52), p. 152

First Point – He was obedient to His parents.
Second Point – *Jesus advanced in wisdom and age and grace.*
Third Point – He seems to have practiced the trade of a carpenter, as St. Mark seems to indicate in Chapter VI: "*Is not this the carpenter?*"

JESUS COMES TO THE TEMPLE AT THE AGE OF TWELVE
(*Luke* 2: 41–50), p. 152

First Point – When Christ our Lord was twelve years old, He went up from Nazareth to Jerusalem.
Second Point – Christ our Lord remained in Jerusalem and His parents did not know it.
Third Point – After three days had passed, they found Him in the Temple, seated in the midst of the doctors and disputing with them. When His parents asked Him where he had been, He replied "*Did you not know that I must be about my Father's business?*"

THE BAPTISM OF CHRIST
(*Matt.* 3: 13–17), p. 153

First Point – After He took leave of His blessed Mother, Christ our Lord, went from Nazareth to the River Jordan where St. John the Baptist was.

Second Point – St. John baptized Christ our Lord. When he wanted to excuse himself, considering that he was unworthy to baptize Him, Christ said to him: "*Let it be so now, for so it becomes us to fulfill all justice.*"

Third Point – The Holy Spirit descended upon Him, and the voice of the Father testified from Heaven: "*This is my beloved Son, in whom I am well pleased.*"

THE TEMPTATION OF CHRIST
(*Luke* 4: 1–13; *Matt.* 4: 1–11), p. 153

First Point – After Jesus was baptized, He went to the desert where he fasted for forty days and forty nights.

Second Point – He was tempted by the enemy three times. *And the tempter came and said to him, "If thou art the Son of God, command that these stones become loaves of bread. . . . Throw thyself down. . . . All these things will I give thee, if thou wilt fall down and worship me.*"

Third Point – *Angels came and ministered to him.*

THE VOCATION OF THE APOSTLES
p. 155

First Point – It appears that St. Peter and St. Andrew were called three times. They were first called to some knowledge, as is shown in the first chapter of St. John [35–42]. They were called a second time to follow Christ in some way, with the intention of returning to the possessions which they had left, as St. Luke relates in Chapter 5: 10–11. The third time they were called to follow Christ our Lord forever, in St. Matthew 4: 18–22 and St. Mark, 1: 16–18.

Second Point – He called Philip, as described in the first chapter of St. John [43], and Matthew, as Matthew himself relates in Chapter 9: 9.

Third Point – He called the other Apostles of whose particular vocation no mention is made in the Gospel.

Three other points are also to be considered:

1. The Apostles were uneducated men, from a low station of life.
2. The dignity to which they were so gently called.
3. The graces and gifts by which they were raised above all the Fathers of the Old and New Testament.

THE FIRST MIRACLE, PERFORMED AT THE MARRIAGE FEAST OF CANA IN GALILEE
(*John* 2: 1–11), p. 157

First Point – Christ our Lord and His disciples were invited to the marriage feast.

Second Point – The Mother calls her Son's attention to the lack of wine, saying: "*They have no wine,*" and she tells the attendants: "*Do whatever he tells you.*"

Third Point – He changed the water into wine . . . *and he manifested his glory, and his disciples believed in him.*

CHRIST DRIVES THE SELLERS OUT OF THE TEMPLE
(*John* 2: 13–16), p. 157

First Point – He drove all of the sellers from the temple with a scourge made of cord.

Second Point – He overturned the tables and scattered the money of the rich money changers that were in the temple.

Third Point – To the poor who were selling doves, He gently said: "*Take these things away, and do not make of the house of my Father a house of business.*"

THE SERMON CHRIST DELIVERED ON THE MOUNT
(*Matt.* 5), p. 158

First Point – He speaks apart to His beloved disciples, about the eight beatitudes: "*Blessed are the poor in spirit . . . the meek . . . the merciful . . . they who mourn . . .*

they who hunger and thirst for justice . . . the clean of heart
. . . . the peacemakers . . . they who suffer persecution."

Second Point — He exhorts them to use their talents well:
"*Even so let your light shine before men, in order that they
may see your good works and give glory to your Father in
heaven.*"

Third Point — He shows that He is not a transgressor of the
law but a fulfiller. He explains the precept not to kill, not to
commit adultery, not to swear falsely, and to love our enemies: "*I say to you, love your enemies, do good to those who
hate you.*"

CHRIST CALMS THE STORM AT SEA
(Matt. 8: 23–27), p. 161

First Point — While Christ our Lord was sleeping in the
boat a great storm arose.

Second Point — His terrified disciples awakened Him; He
reproved them for their little faith, saying to them: "*Why are
you fearful, O you of little faith?*"

Third Point — He commanded the winds and the sea to
cease, at once the wind ceased and the sea became calm. The
men marveled at this, saying: "*What manner of man is this,
that even the wind and the sea obey him?*"

CHRIST WALKS UPON THE SEA
(Matt. 14: 22–33), p. 161

First Point — While Christ our Lord remained upon the
mountain He made His disciples get into the boat, *and when
he had dismissed the crowd He began to pray alone.*

Second Point — The boat was buffeted by the waves, Christ
came to them walking upon the water, and the disciples
thought that it was an apparition.

Third Point — And Christ said to them: "*It is I, fear not.*"
St. Peter, at His command, came to Him, walking upon the
waters, but when he doubted, he began to sink, and Christ
our Lord saved him, and reproved him for his little faith.
Afterwards, when He entered the boat, the wind ceased.

THE APOSTLES ARE SENT FORTH TO PREACH
(*Matt.* 10: 1–16), p. 162

First Point – Christ calls His beloved disciples and gives them power to cast out devils from the bodies of men and to cure all infirmities.

Second Point – He instructs them in prudence and patience. "*Behold, I am sending you forth like sheep in the midst of wolves. Be therefore wise as serpents and guileless as doves.*"

Third Point – He tells them how they are to go: "*Do not keep gold nor silver. Freely you have received, freely give.*" And He tells them what they are to preach: "*And as you go, preach the message, 'The kingdom of heaven is at hand.'*"

THE CONVERSION OF MAGDALENE
(*Luke* 7: 36–50), p. 163

First Point – Magdalene enters the house of the Pharisee, where Christ our Lord is reclining at table. She is carrying an alabaster vessel full of ointment.

Second Point – Standing behind the Lord near His feet, she began to bathe them with her tears and to wipe them with her hair. And she kissed His feet and anointed them with ointment.

Third Point – When the Pharisee accused Magdalene, Christ defended her, saying: "*I say to thee, her sins, many as they are, shall be forgiven her, because she has loved much*" . . . *and he said to the woman:* "*Thy faith has saved thee; go in peace.*"

CHRIST FEEDS FIVE THOUSAND MEN
(*Matt.* 14: 13–21), p. 164

First Point – The disciples asked Christ to dismiss the multitude who were with Him, since it was now late.

Second Point – Christ our Lord commanded them to bring the loaves to Him, and ordered the multitude to sit down to eat. He blessed and broke the loaves and gave them to His disciples and they gave them to the multitude.

Third Point – *And all ate and were satisfied; and they gathered up what was left over, twelve baskets full of fragments.*

THE TRANSFIGURATION OF CHRIST
(Matt. 17: 1–9), p. 165

First Point – Christ our Lord took with Him His beloved disciples Peter, James, and John. *And he was transfigured before them and His face shone as the sun and His garments became white as snow.*

Second Point – He spoke with Moses and Elias.

Third Point – While St. Peter was saying that they should build three tabernacles, a voice from heaven was heard, saying: *"This is my beloved Son . . . hear him."* When the disciples heard this voice, they fell on their faces in great fear. Jesus came and touched them, and said: *"Arise and do not be afraid . . . Tell the vision to no one till the Son of Man has risen from the dead."*

THE RESURRECTION OF LAZARUS
(John 11: 1–45), p. 165

First Point – Martha and Mary make known to Christ our Lord the illness of Lazarus. After Jesus heard of this He remained two days longer in the place where He was, that the miracle might be more evident.

Second Point – Before He raises Lazarus, He asks Martha and Mary to believe, saying: *"I am the resurrection and the life; he who believes in me, even if he die, shall live."*

Third Point – He raises Lazarus after He had wept and said a prayer. The manner of raising him was by the command, *"Lazarus, come forth."*

THE SUPPER IN BETHANY
(Matt. 26: 6–13), p. 168

First Point – Our Lord takes supper in the house of Simon the leper together with Lazarus.

Second Point – Mary pours the precious ointment upon the head of Christ.

Third Point – Judas murmurs, "*To what purpose is this waste of ointment?*" But Jesus again excuses Magdalene, saying: "*Why do you trouble the woman? She has done me a good turn.*"

PALM SUNDAY
(*Matt.* 21: 1–11), p. 169

First Point – Jesus sends for the ass and the colt, saying: "*Loose them and bring them to me, and if anyone say anything to you, you shall say that the Lord hath need of them, and immediately he will send them.*"

Second Point – He mounts the ass which is covered with the garments of the Apostles.

Third Point – The people come forth to meet Him, spreading their garments and branches along the way, saying: "*Hosanna to the Son of David! Blessed is he who comes in the name of the Lord! Hosanna in the highest.*"

JESUS PREACHES IN THE TEMPLE
(*Luke* 19: 47), p. 169

First Point – *And he was teaching daily in the Temple.*

Second Point – After His teaching, since there was no one to receive Him in Jerusalem, He returned to Bethany.

THE LAST SUPPER
(*Matt.* 26: 17–30; *John* 13: 1–30), p. 170

First Point – Jesus ate the Pascal Lamb with His twelve Apostles, to whom He foretold His death: "*Amen I say to you, one of you will betray me.*"

Second Point – He washed the feet of His disciples, even those of Judas. He began with St. Peter, who, considering the majesty of the Lord and his own lowly estate, would not permit it. He said "*Lord, dost thou wash my feet?*" Peter did not understand that Jesus was giving them an example of humility by this. Jesus therefore said to him, "*I have given you an example, that as I have done for you, so you also should do.*"

Third Point – He instituted the most Holy Sacrifice of the Eucharist, as the greatest proof of His love, saying, "*Take and eat.*" When the supper was finished, Judas went forth to sell Christ our Lord.

From the Supper to the Agony in the Garden, Inclusive
(Matt. 26: 30–46; Mark 14: 26–42), p. 173

First Point – After they had finished supper and sung a hymn, our Lord went to Mount Olivet with His disciples, who were full of fear. He left eight of them in Gethsemane, saying to them "*Sit down here while I go yonder and pray.*"

Second Point – Accompanied by Peter, James, and John, He prayed to the Father, saying, "*Father, if it is possible, let this cup pass away from me; yet not as I will, but as thou willest.*" *And falling into an agony he prayed the more earnestly.*

Third Point – So great was the fear that possessed Him, that He said: "*My soul is sad, even unto death*" and he sweated blood so copiously that St. Luke says: "*His sweat became as drops of blood running down upon the ground.*" This supposes that His garments were now saturated with blood.

From the Agony in the Garden to the House of Annas, Inclusive
(Matt. 26: 47–56; Luke 22: 47–53; Mark 14: 43–52; John 18: 1–23), p. 175

First Point – Our Lord allows Himself to be kissed by Judas, and to be seized like a thief. He says to the crowd: "*As against a robber you have come out, with swords and clubs, to seize me. I sat daily with you in the temple teaching, and you did not lay hands on me.*" And when He said: "*whom do you seek?*" His enemies fell to the ground.

Second Point – St. Peter wounded a servant of the high priest. The meek Lord said to him: *"Put back thy sword into its place."* And He healed the servant's wound.

Third Point – Jesus is abandoned by His disciples and dragged before Annas. There St. Peter, who had followed at a distance, denied Him the first time. Then a servant struck Christ in the face, saying to Him: *"Is that the way thou dost answer the high priest?"*

FROM THE HOUSE OF ANNAS TO THE HOUSE OF CAIPHAS, INCLUSIVE
(Matt. 26: 57–75; Mark 14: 53–72; Luke 22: 54–65), p. 178

First Point – Jesus is led bound from the House of Annas to the House of Caiphas where Peter denied Him twice. And when Jesus looked upon Peter, *He went out and wept bitterly.*

Second Point – Jesus was left bound the entire night.

Third Point – And those who held Him prisoner blindfolded Him, and struck Him and buffeted Him, and asked Him, *"Prophesy, who is it that struck thee?"* And in like manner they continued to blaspheme Him.

FROM THE HOUSE OF CAIPHAS TO THE HOUSE OF PILATE, INCLUSIVE
(Matt. 27: 1–26; Luke 23: 1–5; Mark 15: 1–15), p. 182

First Point – The whole multitude of the Jews brought Him before Pilate and accused Him, saying: *"We have found this man perverting the nation, and forbidding the payment of taxes to Caesar."*

Second Point – After Pilate had examined Him several times, he said: *"I find no crime deserving of death in him."*

Third Point – Barabbas the robber was preferred to Him, *The whole mob cried out together saying, "Away with this man, and release to us Barabbas!"*

FROM THE HOUSE OF PILATE TO
THE HOUSE OF HEROD
(*Luke 23: 6–10*), p. 185

First Point–Pilate sent Jesus the Galilean to Herod, the Tetrarch of Galilee.

Second Point–Herod, through curiosity, asked Jesus many questions, but He answered him nothing, even though the scribes and priests unceasingly accused Him.

Third Point–Herod and his entire court mocked Jesus, clothing Him in a white garment.

FROM THE HOUSE OF HEROD TO THAT OF PILATE
(*Matt. 27: 24–30; Luke 23: 12–23
Mark 15: 15–19; John 19: 1–11*), p. 185

First Point–Herod sent Him back to Pilate. Because of this, they became friends, although before this they were enemies.

Second Point–Pilate took Jesus and scourged Him, and the soldiers made a crown of thorns and placed it upon His head. They put a purple cloak about Him, and came before Him, saying: "*Hail, King of the Jews!*" and they struck Him.

Third Point–Pilate had Him brought forth before all the people; *Jesus came forth, wearing the crown of thorns and the purple cloak.* And Pilate said to them: "*Behold the man.*" When they saw Him, the chief priests cried: "*Crucify Him! Crucify Him!*"

FROM THE HOUSE OF PILATE TO
THE CROSS, INCLUSIVE
(*John 19: 12–24*), p. 188

First Point–Pilate, sitting as judge, delivered Jesus to the Jews to be crucified, after they had denied that He was their king, saying: "*We have no king but Caesar.*"

Second Point–He carried the cross upon His shoulders, and as He could not carry it, Simon of Cyrene was forced to carry it after Jesus.

Third Point – They crucified Him between two thieves, placing this title above Him: *Jesus of Nazareth, the King of the Jews.*

JESUS UPON THE CROSS
(*John* 19: 23–37; *Matt.* 27: 35–39; *Mark* 15: 24–38; *Luke* 23: 34–46), p. 189

First Point – He spoke seven words on the Cross. He prayed for those who crucified Him; He pardoned the thief; He entrusted His Mother to St. John; He said in a loud voice: "*I thirst,*" and they gave Him gall and vinegar; He said that He was forsaken; He said: "*It is consummated!*"; He said: "*Father, into thy hands I commend my spirit.*"

Second Point – The sun was darkened; rocks rent, graves opened; the veil of the temple was torn in two from top to bottom.

Third Point – They blasphemed Him, saying: "*Thou who destroyed the Temple . . . come down from the Cross.*" His garments were divided; His side was pierced with a lance, and blood and water flowed forth.

FROM THE CROSS TO THE SEPULCHER, INCLUSIVE
(*John* 19: 38–42), p. 192

First Point – He was taken down from the Cross by Joseph and Nicodemus in the presence of His sorrowful Mother.

Second Point – His body was carried to the sepulcher, and anointed and buried.

Third Point – Guards were set.

THE RESURRECTION OF CHRIST OUR LORD, AND HIS FIRST APPARITION

First Point – He appeared to the Virgin Mary. Although this is not mentioned in Scripture, it is considered as mentioned when the Scripture says that He appeared to so many others, for the Scripture supposes that we have understanding, as is written "*Are you also without understanding?*"

The Second Apparition
(*Mark 16: 1–11*), p. 193

First Point – Very early in the morning Mary Magdalene, Mary the Mother of Jesus, and Salome go to the tomb. They say to one another: "*Who will roll the stone back from the entrance of the tomb for us.*"

Second Point – They see the stone rolled back and an angel who says: "*You are looking for Jesus of Nazareth . . . he has risen, he is not here.*"

Third Point – He appeared to Mary, who remained near the tomb after the others had departed.

The Third Apparition
(*Matt. 28: 8–10*), p. 193

First Point – These Marys go from the tomb with great fear and joy. They want to announce the resurrection of the Lord to the disciples.

Second Point – Christ our Lord appeared to them on the way, and said to them, "*Hail!*" and they came up to Him, and prostrated themselves at His feet, and adored Him.

Third Point – Jesus said to them: "*Do not be afraid; go, take word to my brethren that they are to set out for Galilee: there they shall see me.*"

The Fourth Apparition
(*Luke 24: 10–12 and 33–34*), p. 194

First Point – When Peter heard from the women that Christ had risen, he hastened to the tomb.

Second Point – He entered the tomb and saw nothing but the linen cloths with which the body of Christ our Lord had been covered.

Third Point – While Peter was thinking about these things, Christ appeared to him. Therefore the Apostles said: "*The Lord is risen indeed, and has appeared to Simon.*"

THE FIFTH APPARITION
(*Luke* 24: 13–35), p. 194

First Point – He appeared to the disciples, who were on the way to Emmaus and were talking of Christ.

Second Point – He reproaches them, and shows them by the Scriptures that Christ had to die and rise again: "*O fool-ish ones and slow of heart to believe in all that the prophets have spoken! Did not Christ have to suffer these things be-fore entering into his glory?*"

Third Point – At their entreaties, He remained with them until He gave them Communion; then He disappeared. And they returned to the disciples and told them how they had known Him in the Communion.

THE SIXTH APPARITION
(*John* 20: 19–23), p. 196

First Point – The disciples, except Thomas, were gathered together, "*for fear of the Jews.*"

Second Point – Jesus appeared to them, the doors being closed, and standing in their midst said: "*Peace be to you.*"

Third Point – He gives them the Holy Spirit saying to them: "*Receive the Holy Spirit; Whose sins you shall forgive, they are forgiven them, and whose sins you shall retain, they are retained.*"

THE SEVENTH APPARITION
(*John* 20: 24–29), p. 196

First Point – Thomas was incredulous since he had not been present at the preceding apparition, and said: "*Unless I see . . . I will not believe.*"

Second Point – Eight days later Jesus appeared to them, the doors being shut, and said to Thomas: "*Bring here thy finger and see . . . and be not unbelieving, but believing.*"

Third Point – Thomas believing, said: "*My Lord and my God.*" And Christ said to him: "*Blessed are they who have not seen, and have believed.*"

The Eighth Apparition
(*John* 21: 1–17), p. 197

First Point – Jesus manifested Himself to seven of His disciples who were fishing. They had been fishing all night and had caught nothing. At His command they cast forth the net *and now they were unable to draw it up for the great number of fishes.*

Second Point – John recognized Him by this miracle, and said to Peter "*It is the Lord.*" Peter cast himself into the sea and came to Christ.

Third Point – He gave them part of a broiled fish and bread to eat. After he had questioned Peter three times on his love for Him, He commended His sheep to him, saying: "*Feed my sheep.*"

The Ninth Apparition
(*Matt.* 28: 16–20), p. 198.

First Point – At the command of the Lord, the disciples went to Mount Thabor.

Second Point – Christ appeared to them, and said: "*All power in heaven and on earth has been given to me.*"

Third Point – He sent them to preach throughout the world, saying: "*Go, therefore, and make disciples of all nations, baptizing them in the name of the Father, and of the Son, and of the Holy Spirit.*"

The Tenth Apparition
(*I Cor. 15: 6*), p. 199

Then he was seen by more than five hundred brethren at one time.

The Eleventh Apparition
(*I Cor. 15: 7*), p. 199

After that he was seen by James.

THE TWELFTH APPARITION

He appeared to Joseph of Arimathea, as may be piously thought, and as we read in the *Lives of the Saints*.

THE THIRTEENTH APPARITION
(*I Cor.* 15: 8), p. 199

After His Ascension He appeared to St. Paul: — *And last of all, as by one born out of due time, he was seen also by me.*

He appeared also in soul to the holy fathers in Limbo, and after He had freed them and taken His body again, He appeared many times to the disciples and discoursed with them.

THE ASCENSION OF CHRIST OUR LORD
(*Acts* 1: 1–11), p. 199

First Point — After Christ our Lord had manifested Himself for forty days to His Apostles, giving them many proofs and signs, and speaking of the Kingdom of God, He commanded them to await in Jerusalem the Holy Spirit that He had promised them.

Second Point — He led them to Mt. Olivet *And He was lifted up before their eyes, and a cloud took Him out of their sight.*

Third Point — While they were looking up to heaven, angels said to them: "*Men of Galilee why do you stand looking up to heaven? This Jesus who has been taken up from you into heaven, shall come in the same way as you have seen him going up to heaven.*"

RULES

RULES FOR THE DISCERNMENT OF SPIRITS

First Week

Rules for perceiving and understanding to some degree the different movements that are produced in the soul—the good, that they may be accepted; the bad, that they may be rejected. These rules are more suitable for the first week.

1. The enemy is accustomed ordinarily to propose apparent pleasure to those persons who go from mortal sin to mortal sin. He thus causes them to imagine sensual delights and pleasure in order to hold them more and more easily and to increase their vices and sins. The good spirit acts in these persons in a contrary way, awakening the conscience to a sense of remorse through the good judgment of their reason.

2. The contrary to the first rule takes place in those who earnestly strive to purify themselves from their sins, and who advance from good to better in the service of God our Lord. Then it is common for the evil spirit to cause anxiety and sadness, and to create obstacles based on false reasoning, through preventing the soul from making further progress. It is characteristic of the good spirit to give courage and strength, consolation, tears, inspiration, and peace, making things easy and removing all obstacles, so that the soul may make further progress in good works.

3. *Spiritual Consolation*. I call it consolation when the soul is aroused by an interior movement which causes it to be inflamed with love of its Creator and Lord, and consequently can love no created thing on the face of the earth for its own sake, but only in the creator of all things. It is likewise consolation when one sheds tears inspired by love of the Lord, whether it be sorrow for sins or because of the Passion of Christ our Lord, or for any other reason that is directly connected to His service and praise. Finally, I call consolation any increase of faith, hope, and charity and any interior joy

that calls and attracts to heavenly things, and to the salvation of one's soul, inspiring it with peace and quiet in Christ our Lord.

4. I call desolation all that is contrary to the third rule, as darkness of the soul, turmoil of the mind, inclination to low and earthly things, restlessness resulting from many disturbances and temptations which lead to loss of faith, loss of hope, and loss of love. It is also desolation when a soul finds itself completely apathetic, tepid, sad, and separated as it were, from its Creator and Lord. For just as consolation is contrary to desolation, so the thoughts that spring from consolation are the opposite of those that spring from desolation.

5. In time of desolation one should never make a change, but stand firm and constant in the resolutions and decision which guided him the day before the desolation, or to the decision which he observed in the preceding consolation. For just as the good spirit guides and consoles us in consolation, so in desolation the evil spirit guides and counsels. Following the counsels of this latter spirit, one can never find the correct way to a right decision.

6. Although in desolation we should not change our earlier resolutions, it will be very advantageous to intensify our activity against the desolation. This can be done by insisting more on prayer, meditation, frequent examinations, and by increasing our penance in some suitable manner.

7. One who is in desolation should consider that our Lord, in order to try him has left him to his own natural powers to resist the different agitations and temptations of the enemy. He can resist with Divine help, which is always available to him, even though he may not clearly perceive it. Although the Lord has withdrawn from him His great fervor, ardent love, and intense grace, He has nevertheless left him sufficient grace for eternal salvation.

8. One who is in desolation must strive to persevere in patience, which is contrary to the vexations that have come upon him. He should consider, also, that consolation will soon return, and strive diligently against the desolation in the manner explained in the sixth rule.

9. *There are three principal reasons why we are in desolation:*

The first is because we are tepid, slothful, or negligent in our Spiritual Exercises, and so through our own fault spiritual consolation is withdrawn from us.

The second is that God may try us to test our worth, and the progress that we have made in His service and praise when we are without such generous rewards of consolation and special graces.

The third is that He may wish to give us a true knowledge and understanding, so that we may truly perceive that it is not within our power to acquire or retain great devotion, ardent love, tears, or any other spiritual consolation, but that all of this is a gift and grace of God our Lord. Nor does God wish us to claim as our own what belongs to another, allowing our intellect to rise up in a spirit of pride or vainglory, attributing to ourselves the devotion or other aspects of spiritual consolation.

10. A person who is in consolation ought to think of how he will conduct himself during the desolation that will follow, and thus build up a new strength for that time.

11. A person who is in consolation should take care to humble and abase himself as much as possible. He should recall how little he is worth in time of desolation without such grace or consolation. On the other hand, a person who is in desolation should recall that he can do much to withstand all of his enemies by using the sufficient grace that he has, and taking strength in his Creator and Lord.

12. The enemy acts like a woman in that he is weak in the presence of strength, but strong if he has his will. For as it is the nature of a woman in a quarrel with a man to lose courage and take to flight when the man makes a show of strength and determination, in like manner, if the man loses courage and begins to flee, the anger, vindictiveness, and rage of the woman become great beyond all bounds. In the same manner it is the nature of our enemy to become powerless, lose courage, and take to flight as soon as a person who is following the spiritual life stands courageously against his temp-

tations and does exactly the opposite to what he suggests. On the contrary, if a person begins to take flight and lose courage while fighting temptation, no wild beast on earth is more fierce than the enemy of our human nature as he pursues his evil intention with ever increasing malice.

13. The enemy also behaves like a false lover who wishes to remain hidden and does not want to be revealed. For when this deceitful man pays court, with evil intent, to the daughter of some good father or the wife of a good husband, he wants his words and suggestions to be kept secret. He is greatly displeased if the girl reveals to her father, or the wife to her husband, his deceitful words and depraved intentions, for he then clearly sees that his plans cannot succeed. In like manner, when the enemy of our human nature tempts a just soul with his wiles and deceits, he wishes and desires that they be received and kept in secret. When they are revealed to a confessor or some other spiritual person who understands his deceits and evil designs, the enemy is greatly displeased for he knows that he cannot succeed in his evil design once his obvious deceits have been discovered.

14. The enemy's behavior is also like that of a military leader who wishes to conquer and plunder the object of his desires. Just as the commander of an army pitches his camp, studies the strength and defenses of a fortress, and then attacks it on its weakest side, in like manner, the enemy of our human nature studies from all sides our theological, cardinal, and moral virtues. Wherever he finds us weakest and most in need regarding our eternal salvation, he attacks and tries to take us by storm.

SECOND WEEK

The following rules will serve for a greater discernment of spirits. They are more applicable to the second week.

1. It belongs to God and His angels to bring true happiness and spiritual joy to the soul and to free it from the sadness and disturbance which the enemy causes. It is the nature of the enemy to fight against such joy and spiritual consola-

tion by proposing [seemingly] serious reasons, subtleties, and continual deceptions.

2. It belongs to God alone to give consolation to the soul without previous cause, for it belongs to the Creator to enter into the soul, to leave it, and to act upon it, drawing it wholly to the love of His Divine Majesty. I say without previous cause, that is, without any previous perception or knowledge of any object from which such consolation might come to the soul through its own acts of intellect and will.

3. When a cause has preceded, both the good angel and the evil one may console the soul but for different purposes. The good angel works for the advancement of the soul, that it may grow and rise to what is more perfect, the evil one consoles for the opposite purpose, that he may draw the soul on to his own evil designs and wickedness.

4. It is characteristic of the evil one to transform himself into an angel of light, to work with the soul in the beginning, but in the end to work for himself. At first he will suggest good and holy thoughts that are in conformity with the disposition of a just soul, then, little by little he strives to gain his own ends by drawing the soul into his hidden deceits and perverse designs.

5. We must pay close attention to the course of our thoughts, and if the beginning, middle, and end are all good and directed to what is entirely right, it is a sign that they are inspired by the good angel. If the course of the thoughts suggested to us ends in something evil, or distracting, or less good than the soul had previously proposed to do; or if these thoughts weaken, disquiet, or disturb the soul by destroying the peace, tranquillity, and quiet which it had before, this is a clear sign that they proceed from the evil spirit, the enemy of our progress, and eternal salvation.

6. When the enemy of our human nature has been detected and recognized by his deceptions and by the bad end to which he leads, it is well for the person who has been tempted to examine afterward the course of the good thoughts that were suggested to him. Let him consider their beginning and how the enemy contrived little by little to make him fall from the state of sweetness and spiritual de-

light that he was enjoying, until he finally brought him to his perverse designs. With the experience and knowledge thus acquired and noted, one may better guard himself in the future against the customary deceits of the enemy.

7. In those who are making spiritual progress, the action of the good angel is gentle, light, and sweet, as a drop of water entering a sponge. The action of the evil spirit is sharp, noisy, and disturbing, like a drop of water falling upon a rock. In those souls that are going from bad to worse, the action of these two spirits is the reverse. The cause for this difference of action is the disposition of the soul, which is either contrary or similar to that of the spirits mentioned above. When the disposition of the soul is contrary to that of the spirits, they enter it with noise and disturbances that are easily perceived. When the disposition of the soul and that of these spirits are similar, they enter silently, as one coming into his own house through an open door.

8. When consolation is without preceding cause, although there is no deception in it, since it proceeds only from God our Lord, as has been stated above, the spiritual person to whom God gives such consolation ought still to consider it with great vigilance and attention. He should carefully distinguish the exact time of such consolation from the time that follows it, during which time the soul continues in fervor and feels the divine favor and the aftereffects of the consolation which has passed. Often in this latter period the soul makes various plans and resolutions which are not inspired directly by God our Lord. They may be the result of its own reflections, in accordance with its own habits, and the consequence of its own concepts or judgments, and they may come either from the good spirit or the evil one. It is therefore necessary that they be very carefully examined before they are given full approval, and are put into action.

RULES FOR THE DISTRIBUTION OF ALMS

The following rules should be followed in the ministry of distributing alms.

1. If I am giving alms to relatives or to friends or to persons to whom I am attracted, I must observe four points which have already been mentioned in part in the matter concerning the choice of a way of life.

a. The love which moves me and inspires me to give the alms must come from above; that is, from the love of God our Lord. I should feel within myself that the greater or less love that I have for these persons is inspired by God, and that he is clearly the source of the reasons for which I love them more.

b. I will picture in my mind a man whom I have never seen or known, and whom I consider to possess the greatest perfection in the office and state of life which he occupies. Now as I would expect such a person to observe a rule of action in the giving of alms that would most contribute to the greater glory of God our Lord and the greater perfection of his own soul. I, too, shall act in the same manner, doing neither more nor less. I shall observe the same role of behavior which I considered to be most perfect for him.

c. I will imagine myself at the point of death and consider the rules of behavior that I should then wish to have followed in fulfilling the duties of my office. Regulating myself accordingly, I will now observe the same standards in my distribution of alms.

d. I will consider that I am at the Day of Judgment and I will reflect on how I should then wish to have fulfilled the duties of my ministry. I will follow now the same rules that I shall then wish to have observed.

2. When anyone feels that he is inclined and attached to those persons to whom he wishes to give alms, he should pause and consider well the four rules given above. He should not give an alms until he has examined and tested his affections and, in conformity with these rules, removed and cast aside all inordinate attachments.

3. There is no wrong in accepting the goods of God our Lord for distribution if one is called to such a ministry by our God and Lord. However, there may easily be fault or excess in the amount and quantity that one ought to keep for his own needs out of that which he holds to give to others. He should therefore reform his life and his state by the rules given above.

4. For these and many other reasons, it is always better and safer, in matters that concern himself and his household, if one retrench and reduce his expenses as much as possible, and thus approach as near as possible our great High Priest, our model and rule, who is Christ our Lord.

In conformity with this doctrine, the Third Council of Carthage, at which St. Augustine was present, decrees and orders that the furniture of a bishop be plain and poor. The same consideration applies to all states of life, making allowance for the condition and rank of each, and observing due proportion. In the married state we have the example of St. Joachim and St. Anne, who divided their means into three parts and gave the first to the poor, the second to the ministry and service of the Temple, and used the third for the support of themselves and their family.

NOTES CONCERNING SCRUPLES

The following notes will be of help in discerning and understanding scruples and the snares of our enemy.

1. The name scruple is ordinarily given to that which proceeds from our judgment and free will; for example, when I freely judge something to be a sin which is not a sin. This might happen when someone, after having accidentally stepped on a cross formed by two straws, of his own accord judges that he has sinned. This is in reality an erroneous judgment and not a real scruple.

2. After I have stepped upon that cross, or after I have thought, said, or done some other thing, the thought comes to me from without that I have sinned, and on the other hand, it seems to me that I have not sinned; nevertheless I am disturbed in this matter, doubting and not doubting that I have sinned. This is truly a scruple and a temptation from our enemy.

3. The first scruple, mentioned in the first note should be much abhorred because it is completely erroneous. But the second type of scruple mentioned in the second note, is for a certain period of time of no little advantage to the soul that devotes itself to spiritual exercises. It may even greatly purify and cleanse such a soul, separating it far from all appearance of sin, according to that saying of St. Gregory: "It is a mark of good souls there to recognize a fault when there is none."

4. The enemy observes very carefully whether one has a delicate or lax conscience. If the conscience is delicate he strives to make it excessively so in order to disturb and ruin it more easily. For example, if the enemy sees that a soul consents to no sin, mortal or venial, or even to the appearance of deliberate sin, since he cannot make the soul fall into what has the appearance of sin, he strives to make it

judge that there is sin where there is none, as in some insignificant word or thought.

If the conscience is lax, the enemy strives to make it still more lax. Thus, if before it took no account of venial sins, he will strive to have it take little account of mortal sins. If before, it did take some account of them, now he will strive that it care much less or not at all about them.

5. The soul that desires to advance in the spiritual life must always take a course contrary to that of the enemy. If the enemy seeks to make the conscience lax, he must strive to make it more sensitive, and if the enemy endeavors to make it delicate to excess, the soul must strive to establish itself solidly in moderation so that it may better maintain its tranquility.

6. When such a good soul wishes to say or do something that is acceptable to the Church and to the mind of our superiors, something that may be for the glory of God our Lord, there may come to it from without, a thought or temptation not to say or do it because it is motivated by vainglory or some other specious reason. On such occasions one must raise his mind to his Creator and Lord, and if he sees that the action is for God's service, or at least not contrary to it, he ought to act in a manner diametrically opposed to the temptation, as St. Bernard answered a like temptation: "I did not begin this because of you, nor because of you will I desist."

RULES FOR THINKING WITH THE CHURCH

In order to have the proper attitude of mind in the Church Militant we should observe the following rules:

1. Putting aside all private judgment, we should keep our minds prepared and ready to obey promptly and in all things the true spouse of Christ our Lord, our Holy Mother, the hierarchical Church.

2. To praise sacramental confession and the reception of the Most Holy Sacrament once a year, and much better once a month, and better still every week, with the requisite and proper dispositions.

3. To praise the frequent hearing of Mass, singing of hymns and psalms, and the recitation of long prayers, both in and out of church; also the hours arranged for fixed times for the whole Divine Office, for prayers of all kinds and for the canonical hours.

4. To praise highly religious life, virginity, and continence; and also matrimony, but not as highly as any of the foregoing.

5. To praise the vows of religion, obedience, poverty, chastity, and other works of perfection and supererogation. It must be remembered that a vow is made in matters that lead to evangelical perfection. It is therefore improper to make a vow in matters that depart from this perfection; as, for example, to enter business, to get married, and so forth.

6. To praise the relics of the saints by venerating them and by praying to these saints. Also to praise the stations, pilgrimages, indulgences, jubilees, Crusade indulgences, and the lighting of candles in the churches.

7. To praise the precepts concerning fasts and abstinences, such as those of Lent, Ember Days, Vigils, Fridays, and Saturdays; likewise to praise acts of penance, both interior and exterior.

8. To praise the adornments and buildings of churches as well as sacred images, and to venerate them according to what they represent.

9. Finally, to praise all the precepts of the Church, holding ourselves ready at all times to find reasons for their defense, and never offending against them.

10. We should be more inclined to approve and praise the directions and recommendations of our superiors as well as their personal behavior. Although sometimes these may not be or may not have been praiseworthy, to speak against them when preaching in public or in conversation with people would give rise to murmuring and scandal rather than to edification. As a result, the people would be angry with their superiors, whether temporal or spiritual. Still, while it does harm to our superiors in their absence to speak ill of them in the presence of the people, it might be useful to speak of their bad conduct to those who can apply a remedy.

11. To praise both positive and scholastic theology, for as it is more characteristic of the positive doctors, such as St. Augustine, St. Jerome, St. Gregory, and others, to encourage the affections to greater love and service of God our Lord in all things, so it also is more characteristic of the scholastic doctors, such as St. Thomas, St. Bonaventure, and the Master of the Sentences, etc., to define and explain for our times the things necessary for eternal salvation, and to refute and expose all errors and fallacies. Also, the scholastic doctors, being of more recent date, not only have a clearer understanding of the Holy Scripture and of the teachings of the positive and holy doctors, but also, being enlightened and inspired by the Divine Power, they are helped by the Councils, Canons, and Constitutions of our Holy Mother Church.

12. We must be on our guard against making comparisons between the living and those who have already gone to their reward, for it is no small error to say, for example: "This man knows more than St. Augustine"; "He is another St. Francis, or even greater"; "He is another St. Paul in goodness, holiness, etc."

13. If we wish to be sure that we are right in all things,

we should always be ready to accept this principle: I will believe that the white that I see is black, if the hierarchical Church so defines it. For, I believe that between the Bridegroom, Christ our Lord, and the Bride, His Church, there is but one spirit, which governs and directs us for the salvation of our souls, for the same Spirit and Lord, who gave us the Ten Commandments, guides and governs our Holy Mother Church.

14. Although it be true that no one can be saved unless it be predestined and unless he have faith and grace, still we must be very careful of our manner of discussing and speaking of these matters.

15. We should not make predestination an habitual subject of conversation. If it is sometimes mentioned we must speak in such a way that no person will fall into error, as happens on occasion when one will say, "It has already been determined whether I will be saved or lost, and in spite of all the good or evil that I do, this will not be changed." As a result, they become apathetic and neglect the works that are conducive to their salvation and to the spiritual growth of their souls.

16. In like manner, we must be careful lest by speaking too much and with too great emphasis on faith, without any distinction or explanation, we give occasion to the people to become indolent and lazy in the performance of good works, whether it be before or after their faith is founded in charity.

17. Also in our discourse we ought not to emphasize the doctrine that would destroy free will. We may therefore speak of faith and grace to the extent that God enables us to do so, for the greater praise of His Divine Majesty. But, in these dangerous times of ours, it must not be done in such a way that good works or free will suffer any detriment or be considered worthless.

18. Although the generous service of God for motives of pure love should be most highly esteemed, we should praise highly the fear of His Divine Majesty, for filial fear and even servile fear are pious and most holy things. When one cannot attain anything better or more useful, this fear

is of great help in rising from mortal sin, and after this first step one easily advances to filial fear which is wholly acceptable and pleasing to God our Lord, since it is inseparable from Divine Love.

APPENDIX

SCRIPTURAL TEXTS FOR THE MEDITATIONS ON THE LIFE OF OUR LORD

The Annunciation of Our Lady
(*Luke 1: 26–38*)

26. Now in the sixth month the angel Gabriel was sent from God to a town of Galilee called Nazareth,

27. to a virgin betrothed to a man named Joseph of the house of David, and the virgin's name was Mary.

28. And when the angel had come to her, he said, "Hail, full of grace, the Lord is with thee. Blessed art thou among women."

29. When she had heard him she was troubled at his word, and kept pondering what manner of greeting this might be.

30. And the angel said to her, "Do not be afraid, Mary, for thou hast found grace with God.

31. Behold, thou shalt conceive in thy womb and shalt bring forth a son; and thou shalt call his name Jesus.

32. He shall be great, and shall be called the Son of the Most High; and the Lord God will give him the throne of David his father, and he shall be king over the house of Jacob forever;

33. and of his kingdom there shall be no end."

34. But Mary said to the angel, "How shall this happen, since I do not know man?"

35. And the angel answered and said to her, "The Holy Spirit shall come upon thee and the power of the Most High shall overshadow thee; and therefore the Holy One to be born shall be called the Son of God.

36. And behold, Elizabeth thy kinswoman also has conceived a son in her old age and she who was called barren is now in her sixth month;

37. for nothing shall be impossible with God."

38. But Mary said, "Behold the handmaid of the Lord; be it done to me according to thy word." And the angel departed from her.

THE VISITATION OF OUR LADY TO ELIZABETH
(*Luke* 1: 39–56)

39. Now in those days Mary arose and went with haste into the hill country, to a town of Juda.

40. And she entered the house of Zachary and saluted Elizabeth.

41. And it came to pass, when Elizabeth heard the greeting of Mary, that the babe in her womb leapt. And Elizabeth was filled with the Holy Spirit,

42. and cried out with a loud voice, saying, "Blessed art thou among women and blessed is the fruit of thy womb!

43. And how have I deserved that the mother of my Lord should come to me?

44. For behold, the moment that the sound of thy greeting came to my ears, the babe in my womb leapt for joy.

45. And blessed is she who has believed, because the things promised her by the Lord shall be accomplished."

46. And Mary said, "My soul magnifies the Lord,

47. and my spirit rejoices in God my Savior;

48. because he has regarded the lowliness of his handmaid; for, behold, henceforth all generations shall call me blessed;

49. because he who is mighty has done great things for me, and holy is his name;

50. and his mercy is from generation to generation on those who fear him.

51. He has shown might with his arms, he has scattered the proud in the conceit of their heart.

52. He has put down the mighty from their thrones, and has exalted the lowly.

53. He has filled the hungry with good things, and the rich he has sent away empty.

54. He has given help to Israel, his servant, mindful of his mercy—

55. Even as he spoke to our father—to Abraham and to his posterity forever."

56. And Mary remained with her about three months and returned to her own house.

THE BIRTH OF CHRIST OUR LORD
(*Luke 2: 1–14*)

1. Now it came to pass in those days, that a decree went forth from Caesar Augustus that a census of the whole world should be taken.

2. This first census took place while Cyrinus was Governor of Syria.

3. And all were going, each to his own town to register.

4. And Joseph also went from Galilee out of the town of Nazareth into Judea to the town of David, which is called Bethlehem—because he was of the house and family of David—

5. to register, together with Mary his espoused wife, who was with child.

6. And it came to pass while they were there, that the days for her to be delivered were fulfilled.

7. And she brought forth her firstborn son, and wrapped him in swaddling clothes, and laid him in a manger, because there was no room for them in the inn.

8. And there were shepherds in the same district living in the fields and keeping watch over their flock by night.

9. And behold, an angel of the Lord stood by them and the glory of God shone round about them, and they feared exceedingly.

10. And the angel said to them, "Do not be afraid, for behold, I bring you good news of great joy which shall be to all the people;

11. for today in the town of David a Savior has been born to you, who is Christ the Lord.

12. And this shall be a sign to you: you will find an infant wrapped in swaddling clothes and lying in a manger."

13. And suddenly there was with the angel a multitude of the heavenly host praising God and saying,

14. "Glory to God in the highest, and on earth peace among men of good will."

THE SHEPHERDS
(*Luke 2: 8–20*)

8. And there were shepherds in the same district living in the fields and keeping watch over their flock by night.

9. And behold, an angel of the Lord stood by them and the glory of God shone round about them, and they feared exceedingly.

10. And the angel said to them, "Do not be afraid, for behold, I bring you good news of great joy which shall be to all the people;

11. for today in the town of David a Savior has been born to you, who is Christ the Lord.

12. And this shall be a sign to you: you will find an infant wrapped in swaddling clothes and lying in a manger."

13. And suddenly there was with the angel a multitude of the heavenly host praising God and saying,

14. "Glory to God in the highest, and on earth peace among men of good will."

15. And it came to pass, when the angels had departed from them into heaven, that the shepherds were saying to one another, "Let us go over to Bethlehem and see this thing that has come to pass, which the Lord has made known to us."

16. So they went with haste, and they found Mary and Joseph and the babe lying in the manger.

17. And when they had seen, they understood what had been told them concerning this child.

18. And all who heard marvelled at the things told them by the shepherds.

19. But Mary kept in mind all these things, pondering them in her heart.

20. And the shepherds returned, glorifying and praising God for all that they had heard and seen, even as it was spoken to them.

The Circumcision
(*Luke 2: 21*)

21. And when eight days were fulfilled for his circumcision his name was called Jesus, the name given him by the angel before he was conceived in the womb.

The Three Magi Kings
(*Matt. 2: 1–12*)

1. Now when Jesus was born in Bethlehem of Judea, in the days of King Herod, behold, Magi came from the East to Jerusalem,

2. saying, "Where is he that is born king of the Jews? For we have seen his star in the East and have come to worship him."

3. But when King Herod heard this, he was troubled, and so was all Jerusalem with him.

4. And gathering together all the chief priests and Scribes of the people, he inquired of them where the Christ was to be born.

5. And they said to him, "In Bethlehem of Judea; for thus it is written by the prophet,

6. And thou, Bethlehem, of the land of Juda, are by no means least among the princes of Juda; for from thee shall come forth a leader who shall rule my people Israel."

7. Then Herod summoned the Magi secretly, and carefully ascertained from them the time when the star had appeared to them.

8. And sending them to Bethlehem, he said, "Go and make careful inquiry concerning the child, and when you have found him bring me word, that I too may go and worship him."

9. Now they, having heard the king, went their way. And behold, the star that they had seen in the East went before them, until it came and stood over the place where the child was.

10. And when they saw the star they rejoiced exceedingly.

11. And entering the house, they found the child with Mary

his mother, and falling down they worshipped him. And opening their treasures they offered him gifts of gold, frankincense and myrrh.

12. And being warned in a dream not to return to Herod, they went back to their own country by another way.

The Purification of Our Lady and the Presentation of the Child Jesus
(*Luke 2: 22–39*)

22. And when the days of her purification were fulfilled according to the Law of Moses, they took him up to Jerusalem to present him to the Lord—

23. as it is written in the Law of the Lord, Every male that opens the womb shall be called holy to the Lord—

24. and to offer a sacrifice according to what is said in the Law of the Lord, "a pair of turtle doves or two young pigeons."

25. And behold, there was in Jerusalem a man named Simeon, and this man was just and devout, looking for the consolation of Israel, and the Holy Spirit was upon him.

26. And it had been revealed to him by the Holy Spirit that he should not see death before he had seen the Christ of the Lord.

27. And he came by inspiration of the Spirit into the temple. And when his parents brought in the child Jesus, to do for him according to the custom of the Law,

28. He also received him into his arms and blessed God, saying,

29. "Now thou dost dismiss thy servant, O Lord, according to thy word, in peace;

30. because my eyes have seen thy salvation,

31. which thou hast prepared before the face of all peoples:

32. a light of revelation to the Gentiles, and a glory for thy people Israel."

33. And his father and mother were marvelling at the things spoken concerning him.

34. And Simeon blessed them, and said to Mary his mother,

"Behold, this child is destined for the fall and for the rise of many in Israel, and for a sign that shall be contradicted.
35. And thy own soul a sword shall pierce, that the thoughts of many hearts may be revealed."
36. There was also Anna, a prophetess, daughter of Phanuel, of the tribe of Aser. She was of a great age, having lived with her husband seven years from her maidenhood,
37. And by herself as a widow to eighty-four years. She never left the temple, with fastings and prayers worshipping night and day.
38. And coming up at that very hour, she began to give praise to the Lord, and spoke of him to all who were awaiting the redemption of Jerusalem.
39. And when they had fulfilled all things prescribed in the Law of the Lord, they returned to Galilee, into their own town of Nazareth.

THE FLIGHT INTO EGYPT
(Matt. 2: 13–15)

13. But when they had departed, behold, an angel of the Lord appeared in a dream to Joseph, saying, "Arise, and take the child and his mother, and flee into Egypt, and remain there until I tell thee. For Herod will seek the child to destroy him."
14. So he arose, and took the child and his mother by night, and withdrew into Egypt.
15. And remained there until the death of Herod; that what was spoken by the Lord through the prophet might be fulfilled, Out of Egypt I called my son.

THE RETURN FROM EGYPT
(Matt. 2: 19–23)

19. But when Herod was dead, behold, an angel of the Lord appeared in a dream to Joseph in Egypt,
20. saying, "Arise and take the child and his mother, and go into the land of Israel, for those who sought the child's life are dead."

21. So he arose and took the child and his mother, and went into the land of Israel.

22. But hearing that Archelaus was reigning in Judea in place of his father Herod, he was afraid to go there; and being warned in a dream, he withdrew into the region of Galilee.

23. And he went and settled in a town called Nazareth; that there might be fulfilled what was spoken through the prophets, He shall be called a Nazarene.

THE LIFE OF OUR LORD FROM THE AGE OF
TWELVE TO THE AGE OF THIRTY
(*Luke 2: 51–52*)

51. And he went down with them and came to Nazareth, and was subject to them; and his mother kept all these things carefully in her heart.

52. And Jesus advanced in wisdom and age and grace before God and men.

JESUS COMES TO THE TEMPLE
AT THE AGE OF TWELVE
(*Luke 2: 41–50*)

41. And his parents were wont to go every year to Jerusalem at the Feast of the Passover.

42. And when he was twelve years old they went up to Jerusalem according to the custom of the feast.

43. And after they had fulfilled the day, when they were returning, the boy Jesus remained in Jerusalem, and his parents did not know it.

44. But thinking that he was in the caravan, they had come a day's journey before it occurred to them to look for him among their relatives and acquaintances.

45. And not finding him, they returned to Jerusalem in search of him.

46. And it came to pass after three days, that they found him in the temple, sitting in the midst of the teachers, listening to them and asking them questions.

47. And all who were listening to him were amazed at his understanding and his answers.

48. And when they saw him, they were astonished. And his mother said to him, "Son, why hast thou done so to us? Behold, in sorrow thy father and I have been seeking thee."

49. And he said to them, "How is it that you sought me? Did you not know that I must be about my Father's business?"

50. And they did not understand the word that he spoke to them.

THE BAPTISM OF CHRIST
(*Matt.* 3: 13–17)

13. Then Jesus came from Galilee to John, at the Jordan, to be baptized by him.

14. And John was for hindering him, and said, "It is I who ought to be baptized by thee, and dost thou come to me?"

15. But Jesus answered and said to him, "Let it be so now, for so it becomes us to fulfill all justice." Then, he permitted him.

16. And when Jesus had been baptized, he immediately came up from the water. And behold, the heavens were opened to him, and he saw the Spirit of God descending as a dove and coming upon him.

17. And behold, a voice from the heavens said, "This is my beloved Son, in whom I am well pleased."

THE TEMPTATION OF CHRIST
(*Luke* 4: 1–13)

1. Now Jesus full of the Holy Spirit, returned from the Jordan, and was led by the Spirit about the desert

2. for forty days being tempted the while by the devil. And he ate nothing those days; and when they were completed he was hungry.

3. And the Devil said to him, "If thou art the Son of God, command that this stone become a loaf of bread."

4. And Jesus answered him, "It is written, Not by bread alone shall man live, but by every word of God."

5. And the devil led him up, and showed him all the kingdoms of the world in a moment of time.

6. And he said to him, "To thee will I give all this power and their glory; for to me they have been delivered, and to whomever I will I give them.

7. Therefore if thou wilt worship before me, the whole shall be thine."

8. And Jesus answered and said to him, "It is written, The Lord thy God shalt thou worship and him only shalt thou serve."

9. Then he led him to Jerusalem and set him on the pinnacle of the temple and said to him, "If thou art the Son of God, throw thyself down from here;

10. for it is written, "He will give his angels charge concerning thee, to preserve thee;

11. and upon their hands they shall bear thee up, lest thou dash thy foot against a stone."

12. And Jesus answered and said to him, "It is said, Thou shalt not tempt the Lord thy God."

13. And when the devil had tried every temptation, he departed from him for a while.

(Matt. 4: 1–11)

1. Then Jesus was led into the desert by the Spirit, to be tempted by the devil.

2. And after fasting forty days and forty nights, he was hungry.

3. And the tempter came and said to him, "If thou art the Son of God, command that these stones become loaves of bread."

4. But he answered and said, "It is written Not by bread alone does man live, but by every word that comes forth from the mouth of God."

5. Then the devil took him into the holy city and set him on the pinnacle of the temple.

6. And said to him, "If thou are the Son of God, throw

thyself down; for it is written, He will give his angels charge concerning thee; and upon their hands they shall bear thee up, lest thou dash thy foot against a stone."

7. Jesus said to him, "It is written further, Thou shalt not tempt the Lord thy God."

8. Again the devil took him to a very high mountain, and showed him all the kingdoms of the world and the glory of them.

9. And he said to him, "All these things will I give thee if thou wilt fall down and worship me."

10. Then Jesus said to him, "Begone Satan! for it is written, The Lord thy God shalt thou worship and him only shalt thou serve."

11. Then the devil left him; and behold, angels came and ministered to him.

THE VOCATION OF THE APOSTLES
(John 1: 35–42)

35. Again the next day John was standing there, and two of his disciples.

36. And looking upon Jesus as he walked by, he said, "Behold the lamb of God!"

37. And the two disciples heard him speak, and they followed Jesus.

38. But Jesus turned round, and seeing them following him, said to them, "What is it you seek?" They said to him, "Rabbi (which interpreted means Master), where dwellest thou?"

39. He said to them, "Come and see." They came and saw where he was staying; and they stayed with him that day. It was about the tenth hour.

40. Now Andrew, the brother of Simon Peter, was one of the two who had heard John and had followed him.

41. He found first his brother Simon and said to him, "We have found the Messias (which interpreted is Christ)."

42. And he led him to Jesus. But Jesus, looking upon him, said, "Thou art Simon, the son of John; thou shalt be called Cephas (which interpreted is Peter)."

(Luke 5: 10–11)

10. And so were also James and John, the sons of Zebedee, who were partners with Simon. And Jesus said to Simon, "Do not be afraid; henceforth thou shalt catch men."
11. And when they had brought their boats to land, they left all and followed him.

(Matt. 4: 18–22)

18. And he was walking by the sea of Galilee, he saw two brothers, Simon who was called Peter, and his brother Andrew, casting a net into the sea (for they were fishermen).
19. And he said to them, "Come, follow me, and I will make you fishers of men."
20. And at once they left the nets, and followed him.
21. And going farther on, he saw two other brothers, James the son of Zebedee, and his brother John, in a boat with Zebedee their father, mending their nets; and he called them.
22. And immediately they left their nets and their father, and followed him.

(Mark 1: 16–18)

16. And passing along by the sea of Galilee, he saw Simon and his brother Andrew, casting their nets into the sea (for they were fishermen).
17. And Jesus said to them, "Come, follow me, and I will make you fishers of men."
18. And at once they left the nets, and followed him.

(John 1: 43)

43. The next day he was about to leave for Galilee, and he found Philip. And Jesus said to him, "Follow me."

(Matt. 9: 9)

9. Now as Jesus passed on from there, he saw a man named Matthew sitting in the tax-collector's place, and said to him, "Follow me." And he arose and followed him.

THE FIRST MIRACLE, PERFORMED AT THE MARRIAGE FEAST OF CANA IN GALILEE
(John 2: 1–11)

1. And on the third day a marriage took place at Cana of Galilee, and the mother of Jesus was there.
2. Now Jesus too was invited to the marriage, and also his disciples.
3. And the wine having run short, the mother of Jesus said to him, "They have no wine."
4. And Jesus said to her, "What wouldst thou have me do, woman? My hour has not yet come."
5. His mother said to the attendants, "Do whatever he tells you."
6. Now six stone water-jars were placed there after the Jewish manner of purification, each holding two or three measures.
7. Jesus said to them, "Fill the jars with water." And they filled them to the brim.
8. And Jesus said to them, "Draw out now, and take to the chief steward." And they took it to him.
9. Now when the chief steward had tasted the water after it had become wine, not knowing when it was (though the attendants who had drawn the water knew), the chief steward called the bridegroom,
10. and said to him, "Every man at first sets forth the good wine, and when they have drunk freely, then that which is poorer. But thou hast kept the good wine until now."
11. This first of his signs Jesus worked at Cana of Galilee; and he manifested his glory, and his disciples believed in him.

CHRIST DRIVES THE SELLERS OUT OF THE TEMPLE
(John 2: 13–16)

13. Now the Passover of the Jews was at hand, and Jesus went up to Jerusalem.
14. And he found in the temple men selling oxen, sheep and doves, and money-changers at their tables.

15. And making a kind of whip of cords, he drove them all out of the temple, also the sheep and oxen, and he poured out the money of the changers and overturned the tables. 16. And to them who were selling the doves he said, "Take these things away, and do not make the house of my Father a house of business."

THE SERMON CHRIST DELIVERED ON THE MOUNT
(Matt. 5)

1. And seeing the crowds, he went up the mountain. And when he was seated, his disciples came to him.

2. And opening his mouth he taught them, saying,

3. Blessed are the poor in spirit, for theirs is the kingdom of heaven.

4. Blessed are the meek, for they shall possess the earth.

5. Blessed are they who mourn, for they shall be comforted.

6. Blessed are they who hunger and thirst for justice, for they shall be satisfied.

7. Blessed are the merciful, for they shall obtain mercy.

8. Blessed are the clean of heart, for they shall see God.

9. Blessed are the peacemakers, for they shall be called Children of God.

10. Blessed are they who suffer persecution for justice' sake, for theirs is the kingdom of heaven.

11. Blessed are you when men reproach you, and persecute you, and, speaking falsely, say all manner of evil against you, for my sake.

12. Rejoice and exult, because your reward is great in heaven; for so did they persecute the prophets who were before you.

13. You are the salt of the earth; but if the salt loses its strength, what shall it be salted with? It is no longer of any use but to be thrown out and trodden underfoot by men.

14. You are the light of the world. A city set on a mountain cannot be hidden.

15. Neither do men light a lamp and put it under the measure, but upon the lamp-stand, so as to give light to all in the house.

16. Even so let your light shine before men, in order that they may see your good works and give glory to your Father in heaven.

17. Do not think that I have come to destroy the Law or the Prophets. I have not come to destroy, but to fulfill.

18. For amen I say to you, till heaven and earth pass away, not one jot or one tittle shall be lost from the Law till all things have been accomplished.

19. Therefore whoever does away with one of these least commandments, and so teaches men, shall be called least in the kingdom of heaven; but whoever carries them out and teaches them, he shall be called great in the kingdom of heaven.

20. For I say to you that unless your justice exceeds that of the Scribes and Pharisees, you shall not enter the kingdom of heaven.

21. "You have heard that it was said to the ancients, 'Thou shalt not kill'; and that whoever shall kill shall be liable to judgment.

22. But I say to you that everyone who is angry with his brother shall be liable to judgment; and whoever says to his brother, 'Raca,' shall be liable to the Sanhedrin; and whoever says, 'Thou fool!', shall be liable to the fire of Gehenna.

23. Therefore, if thou art offering thy gift at the altar, and there rememberest that thy brother has anything against thee,

24. leave thy gift before the altar and go first to be reconciled to thy brother, and then come and offer thy gift.

25. Come to terms with thy opponent quickly while thou art with him on the way; lest thy opponent deliver thee to the judge, and the judge to the officer, and thou be cast into prison.

26. Amen I say to thee, thou wilt not come out from it until thou hast paid the last penny.

27. "You have heard that it was said to the ancients, 'Thou shalt not commit adultery.'

28. But I say to you that anyone who so much as looks with lust at a woman has already committed adultery with her in his heart.

29. So if thy right eye is an occasion of sin to thee, pluck it out and cast it from thee; for it is better for thee that one of thy members should perish than that thy whole body should be thrown in hell.

30. And if thy right hand is an occasion of sin to thee, cut it off and cast it from thee; for it is better for thee that one of thy members should be lost than that thy whole body should go into hell.

31. "It was said moreover, 'Whoever puts away his wife, let him give her a written notice of dismissal.'

32. But I say to you that everyone who puts away his wife, save on account of immorality, causes her to commit adultery; and he who marries a woman who has been put away commits adultery.

33. "Again you have heard that it was said to the ancients, 'Thou shalt not swear falsely, but fulfill thy oaths to the Lord.'

34. But I say to you not to swear at all; neither by heaven, for it is the throne of God;

35. Nor by the earth for it is His footstool; nor by Jerusalem, for it is the city of the great King.

36. Neither do thou swear by thy head, for thou canst not make one hair white or black.

37. But let your speech be, 'Yes, yes'; 'No, no'; and whatever is beyond these comes from the evil one.

38. "You have heard that it was said, 'An eye for an eye,' and 'A tooth for a tooth.'

39. But I say to you not to resist the evildoer; on the contrary, if someone strike thee on the right cheek, turn to him the other also;

40. And if anyone would go to law with thee and take thy tunic, let him take thy cloak as well;

41. and whoever forces thee to go for one mile, go with him two.

42. To him who asks of thee, give; and from him who would borrow of thee, do not turn away.

43. "You have heard that it was said, 'Thou shalt love thy neighbor, and shalt hate thy enemy.'

44. But I say to you, love your enemies, do good to those who hate you, and pray for those who persecute and calumniate you,

45. so that you may be children of your Father in heaven, who makes his sun to rise on the good and the evil, and sends rain on the just and the unjust.

46. For if you love those that love you, what reward shall you have? Do not even the publicans do that?

47. And if you salute your brethren only, what are you doing more than others? Do not even the Gentiles do that?

48. You therefore are to be perfect, even as your heavenly Father is perfect.

CHRIST CALMS THE STORM AT SEA
(*Matt.* 8: 23–27)

23. Then he got into a boat and his disciples followed him.

24. And behold, there arose a great storm on the sea, so that the boat was covered by the waves; but he was asleep.

25. So they came and woke him, saying, "Lord save us! we are perishing!"

26. But he said to them, "Why are you fearful, O you of little faith?" Then he arose and rebuked the wind and the sea, and there came a great calm.

27. And the men marvelled, saying, "What manner of man is this, that even the wind and the sea obey him?"

CHRIST WALKS UPON THE SEA
(*Matt.* 14: 22–33)

22. And immediately afterwards he made his disciples get into the boat and cross the sea ahead of him, while he dismissed the crowd.

23. And when he had dismissed the crowd, he went up the mountain by himself to pray. And when it was late, he was there alone.

24. And the boat was in the midst of the sea, buffeted by the waves, for the wind was against them.

25. But in the fourth watch of the night he came to them, walking upon the sea.

26. And they, seeing him walking upon the sea, were greatly alarmed, and exclaimed, "It is a ghost!" and they cried out for fear.

27. Then Jesus immediately spoke to them, saying, "Take courage; it is I, do not be afraid."

28. But Peter answered him and said, "Lord, if it is thou, bid me come to thee over the water."

29. And he said, "Come." Then Peter got out of the boat and walked on the water to come to Jesus.

30. But seeing the wind was strong, he was afraid; and as he began to sink he cried out saying, "Lord save me!"

31. And Jesus at once stretched forth his hand and took hold of him, saying to him, "O thou of little faith, why didst thou doubt?"

32. And when they got into the boat the wind fell.

33. But they who were in the boat came and worshipped him saying, "Truly thou art the Son of God."

THE APOSTLES ARE SENT FORTH TO PREACH
(*Matt.* 10: 1–16)

1. Then having summoned his twelve disciples, he gave them power over unclean spirits, to cast them out, and to cure every kind of disease and infirmity.

2. Now these are the names of the twelve apostles: first Simon, who is called Peter, and his brother Andrew;

3. James the son of Zebedee, and his brother John; Philip and Bartholomew; Thomas and Matthew the publican; James the son of Alpheus, and Thaddeus;

4. Simon the Cananean, and Judas Iscariot, he who betrayed him.

5. These twelve Jesus sent forth having instructed them thus: "Do not go in the direction of the Gentiles, nor enter the town of Samaritans;

6. But go rather to the lost sheep of the house of Israel.

7. And as you go, preach the message, 'The kingdom of heaven is at hand!'

8. Cure the sick, raise the dead, cleanse the lepers, cast out devils. Freely you have received, freely give.

9. Do not keep gold, or silver, or money in your girdles,
10. no wallet for your journey, nor two tunics, nor sandals, nor staff; for the laborer deserves his living.
11. And whatever town or village you enter, enquire who in it is worthy; and stay there until you leave.
12. As you enter the house, salute it.
13. If then that house be worthy, your peace will come upon it; but if it be not worthy, let your peace return to you.
14. And whoever does not receive you, or listen to your words—go forth outside that house or town, and shake off the dust from your feet.
15. Amen I say to you, it will be more tolerable for the land of Sodom and Gomorrah in the day of judgment than for that town.
16. Behold, I am sending you forth like sheep in the midst of wolves. Be therefore wise as serpents, and guileless as doves."

THE CONVERSION OF MAGDALENE
(*Luke 7: 36–50*)

36. Now one of the Pharisees asked him to dine with him; so he went into the house of the Pharisee and reclined at table.
37. And behold, a woman in the town who was a sinner, upon learning that he was at table in the Pharisee's house, brought an alabaster jar of ointment;
38. and standing behind him at his feet, she began to bathe his feet with her tears, and wiped them with the hair of her head, and kissed his feet, and anointed them with ointment.
39. Now when the Pharisee, who had invited him, saw it, he said to himself, "This man, were he a prophet, would surely know who and what manner of woman this is who is touching him, for she is a sinner."
40. And Jesus answered and said to him, "Simon, I have something to say to thee." And he said, "Master, speak."
41. "A certain money-lender had two debtors; the one owed five hundred denarii, the other fifty.

42. As they had no means of paying, he forgave them both. Which of them, therefore, will love him more?"

43. Simon answered and said, "He, I suppose, to whom he forgave more." And he said to him, "Thou hast judged rightly."

44. And turning to the woman, he said to Simon, "Dost thou see this woman? I came into thy house; thou gavest me no water for my feet; but she has bathed my feet with tears, and has wiped them with her hair.

45. Thou gavest me no kiss; but she, from the moment she entered, has not ceased to kiss my feet.

46. Thou didst not anoint my head with oil; but she has anointed my feet with ointment.

47. Wherefore I say to thee, her sins, many as they are, shall be forgiven her, because she has loved much. But he to whom little is forgiven, loves little."

48. And he said to her, "Thy sins are forgiven."

49. And they who were at table with him began to say within themselves, "Who is this man, who even forgives sins?"

50. But he said to the woman, "Thy faith has saved thee; go in peace."

CHRIST FEEDS FIVE THOUSAND MEN
(*Matt.* 14: 13–21)

13. When Jesus heard this, he withdrew by boat to a desert place apart; but the crowds heard of it and followed him on foot from the towns.

14. And when he landed, he saw a large crowd, and out of compassion for them he cured their sick.

15. Now when it was evening, his disciples came to him, saying, "This is a desert place and the hour is already late; send the crowds away, so that they may go into the villages and buy themselves food."

16. But Jesus said to them, "They do not need to go away; you yourselves give them some food."

17. They answered him, "We have here only five loaves and two fishes."

18. He said to them, "Bring them here to me."

19. And when he had ordered the crowd to recline on the grass, he took the five loaves and the two fishes, and looking up to heaven, blessed and broke the loaves, and gave them to his disciples, and the disciples gave them to the crowds.

20. And all ate and were satisfied; and they gathered up what was left over, twelve baskets full of fragments.

21. Now the number of those who had eaten was five thousand men, without counting women and children.

THE TRANSFIGURATION OF CHRIST
(*Matt. 17: 1–9*)

1. Now after six days Jesus took Peter, James and his brother John, and led them up a high mountain by themselves,

2. And was transfigured before them. And his face shone as the sun, and his garments became white as snow.

3. And behold, there appeared to them Moses and Elias talking together with him.

4. Then Peter addressed Jesus saying, "Lord, it is good for us to be here. If thou wilt, let us set up three tents here, one for thee, one for Moses, and one for Elias."

5. As he was still speaking, behold a bright cloud overshadowed them, and behold a voice out of the cloud said, "This is my beloved Son, in whom I am well pleased; hear him."

6. And on hearing it the disciples fell on their faces and were exceedingly afraid.

7. And Jesus came near and touched them, and said to them, "Arise, and do not be afraid."

8. But lifting up their eyes, they saw no one but Jesus only.

9. And as they were coming down from the mountain, Jesus cautioned them, saying, "Tell the vision to no one, till the Son of Man has risen from the dead."

THE RESURRECTION OF LAZARUS
(*John 11: 1–45*)

1. Now a certain man was sick, Lazarus of Bethany, the village of Mary and her sister Martha.

2. Now it was Mary who anointed the Lord with ointment, and wiped his feet dry with her hair, whose brother Lazarus was sick.

3. The sisters therefore sent to him, saying, "Lord, behold, he whom thou lovest is sick."

4. But when Jesus heard this, he said to them, "This sickness is not unto death, but for the glory of God, that through it the Son of God may be glorified."

5. Now Jesus loved Martha and her sister Mary, and Lazarus.

6. So when he heard that he was sick, he remained two more days in the same place.

7. Then afterwards he said to his disciples, "Let us go again into Judea."

8. The disciples said to him, "Rabbi, just now the Jews were seeking to stone thee; and dost thou go there again?"

9. Jesus answered, "Are there not twelve hours in the day? If a man walks in the day, he does not stumble, because he sees the light of this world.

10. But if he walks in the night, he stumbles, because the light is not in him."

11. These things he spoke, and after this he said to them, "Lazarus, our friend, sleeps. But I go that I may wake him from sleep."

12. His disciples therefore said, "Lord, if he sleeps he will be safe."

13. Now Jesus had spoken of his death, but they thought he was speaking of the repose of sleep.

14. So then Jesus said to them plainly, "Lazarus is dead;

15. And I rejoice on your account that I was not there, that you may believe. But let us go to him."

16. Thomas, who is called the Twin, said therefore to his fellow-disciples, "Let us also go, that we may die with him."

17. Jesus therefore came and found him already four days in the tomb.

18. Now Bethany was close to Jerusalem, some fifteen stadia distant.

19. And many of the Jews had come to Martha and Mary, to comfort them on account of their brother.

20. When, therefore, Martha heard that Jesus was coming, she went to meet him. But Mary remained at home.

21. Martha therefore said to Jesus, "Lord, if thou hadst been here my brother would not have died.

22. But even now I know that whatever thou shalt ask of God, God will give it to thee."

23. Jesus said to her, "Thy brother shall rise."

24. Martha said to him, "I know that he will rise at the resurrection, on the last day."

25. Jesus said to her, "I am the resurrection and the life; he who believes in me, even if he die, shall live;

26. and whoever lives and believes in me, shall never die. Dost thou believe this?"

27. She said to him, "Yes, Lord, I believe that thou are the Christ, the Son of God, who hast come into the world."

28. And when she had said this, she went away and quietly called Mary her sister, saying, "The Master is here and calls thee."

29. As soon as she heard this, she rose quickly and came to him,

30. for Jesus had not yet come into the village, but was still at the place where Martha had met him.

31. When, therefore, the Jews, who were with her in the house and were comforting her, saw Mary rise up quickly and go out, they followed her, saying, "She is going to the tomb to weep there."

32. When, therefore, Mary came where Jesus was, and saw him, she fell at his feet, and said to him, "Lord, if thou hadst been here, my brother would not have died."

33. When, therefore, Jesus saw her weeping, and the Jews who had come with her weeping, he groaned in spirit and was troubled,

34. and said, "Where have you laid him?" They said to him, "Lord, come and see."

35. And Jesus wept.

36. The Jews therefore said, "See how he loved him."

37. But some of them said, "Could not he who opened the eyes of the blind, have caused that this man should not die?"

38. Jesus therefore, again groaning in himself, came to the tomb. Now it was a cave, and a stone was laid against it.

39. Jesus said, "Take away the stone." Martha, the sister of him who was dead, said to him, "Lord by this time he is already decayed, for he is dead four days."

40. Jesus said to her, "Have I not told thee that if thou believe thou shalt behold the glory of God?"

41. They therefore removed the stone. And Jesus raising his eyes, said, "Father, I give thee thanks for thou hast heard me.

42. Yet, I knew that thou always hearest me; but because of the people who stand round, I spoke, that they may believe that thou hast sent me."

43. When he had said this, he cried out with a loud voice, "Lazarus come forth!"

44. And at once he who had been dead came forth, bound feet and hands with bandages, and his face was tied up with a cloth. Jesus said to them, "Unbind him, and let him go."

45. Many therefore of the Jews who had come to Mary, and had seen what he did, believed in him.

THE SUPPER IN BETHANY
(Matt. 26: 6–13)

6. Now when Jesus was in Bethany, in the house of Simon the Leper,

7. a woman came up to him with an alabaster jar of precious ointment, and she poured it on his head, as he reclined at table.

8. But when the disciples saw this, they were indignant, and said, "To what purpose is this waste?

9. For this might have been sold for much and given to the poor."

10. But Jesus perceiving it, said to them, "Why do you trouble the woman? She has done me a good turn.

11. For the poor you have always with you, but you do not always have me.

12. For in pouring this ointment on my body, she has done it for my burial.

13. Amen I say to you, wherever in the whole world this gospel is preached, this also that she has done shall be told in memory of her.

PALM SUNDAY
(*Matt.* 21: 1–11)

1. And when they drew near to Jerusalem, and came to Bethphage, on the Mount of Olives, then Jesus sent two disciples,
2. saying to them, "Go into the village opposite you, and immediately you will find an ass tied, and a colt with her; loose them and bring them to me.
3. And if anyone say anything to you, you shall say that the Lord has need of them, and immediately he will send them."
4. Now this was done that what was spoken through the prophet might be fulfilled.
5. Tell the daughter of Sion: Behold thy king comes to thee, meek and seated upon an ass, and upon a colt, the foal of a beast of burden.
6. So the disciples went and did as Jesus had directed them.
7. And they brought the ass and the colt, laid their cloaks on them, and made him sit thereon.
8. And most of the crowd spread their cloaks upon the road, while others were cutting branches from the trees, and strewing them on the road.
9. And the crowd that went before him, and those that followed, kept crying out, saying, *Hosanna to the Son of David! Blessed is he who comes in the name of the Lord! Hosanna in the highest!*
10. And when he entered Jerusalem, all the city was thrown into commotion, saying, "Who is this?"
11. But the crowds kept on saying, "This is Jesus the prophet from Nazareth of Galilee."

JESUS PREACHES IN THE TEMPLE
(*Luke* 19: 47)

47. And he was teaching daily in the temple. But the chief priests and the Scribes and the leading men of the people sought to destroy him.

The Last Supper
(*Matt.* 26: 17–30)

17. Now on the first day of the Unleavened Bread, the disciples came to Jesus and said, "Where dost thou want us to prepare for thee to eat the passover?"

18. But Jesus said, "Go into the city to a certain man, and say to him, 'The Master says, My time is near at hand; at thy house I am keeping the Passover with my disciples.'"

19. And the disciples did as Jesus bade them, and prepared the Passover.

20. Now when evening arrived, he reclined at table with the twelve disciples.

21. And while they were eating he said, "Amen I say to you, one of you is about to betray me."

22. And they being very much troubled, began every one to say: "Is it I, Lord?"

23. But he answering, said: "He that dippeth his hand with me in the dish, he shall betray me.

24. The Son of man indeed goeth, as it is written of him: but woe to that man by whom the Son of man shall be betrayed: it were better for him, if that man had not been born."

25. And Judas that betrayed him, answering said: "Is it I, Rabbi?" He saith to him: "Thou hast said it."

26. And whilst they were at supper, Jesus took bread, and blessed, and broke: and gave to his disciples, and said: "Take ye, and eat. This is my body."

27. And taking the chalice, he gave thanks, and gave to them, saying: "Drink ye all of this.

28. For this is my blood of the new testament, which shall be shed for many unto remission of sins.

29. And I say to you, I will not drink from henceforth of this fruit of the vine, until that day when I shall drink it with you new in the kingdom of my Father."

30. And a hymn being said, they went out unto Mount Olivet.

(John 13: 1–30)

1. Before the feast of the Passover, Jesus knowing that the hour had come for him to pass out of this world to the Father, having loved his own who were in the world, loved them to the end.

2. And during the supper, the devil having already put it into the heart of Judas Iscariot, the son of Simon, to betray him, Jesus,

3. knowing that the Father had given all things into his hands, and that he had come forth from God and was going to God,

4. rose from the supper and laid aside his garments, and taking a towel girded himself.

5. Then he poured water into the basin and began to wash the feet of the disciples, and to dry them with the towel with which he was girded.

6. He came then to Simon Peter. And Peter said to him, "Lord, dost thou wash my feet?"

7. Jesus answered and said to him, "What I do thou knowest not now; but thou shalt know hereafter."

8. Peter said to him, "Thou shalt never wash my feet!" Jesus answered him, "If I do not wash thee, thou shall have no part with me."

9. Simon Peter said to him, "Lord, not my feet only, but also my hands and my head!"

10. Jesus said to him, "He who has bathed needs only to wash, he is clean all over. And you are clean, but not all."

11. For he knew who it was that would betray him. This is why he said, "You are not all clean."

12. Now after he had washed their feet and put on his garments, when he had reclined again, he said to them, "Do you know what I have done to you?

13. You call me Master and Lord, and you say well, for so I am.

14. If, therefore, I the Lord and Master have washed your feet, you also ought to wash the feet of one another.

15. For I have given you an example, that as I have done to you, so you also should do.

16. Amen, amen, I say to you, no servant is greater than his master, nor is one who is sent greater than he who sent him.

17. If you know these things, blessed shall you be if you do them.

18. I do not speak of you all. I know whom I have chosen; but that the Scripture may be fulfilled, He who eats bread with me has lifted up his heel against me.

19. I tell you now before it comes to pass, that when it has come to pass you may believe that I am he.

20. Amen, amen, I say to you, he who receives anyone I send, receives me; and he who receives me, receives him who sent me."

21. When Jesus had said these things he was troubled in spirit, and said solemnly, "Amen, amen, I say to you, one of you will betray me."

22. The disciples therefore looked at one another, uncertain of whom he was speaking.

23. Now one of his disciples he whom Jesus loved was reclining at Jesus' bosom.

24. Simon Peter therefore beckoned to him, and said to him, "Who is it of whom he speaks?"

25. He therefore, leaning back upon the bosom of Jesus, said to him, "Lord, who is it?"

26. Jesus answered, "It is he for whom I shall dip the bread and give it to him." And when he had dipped the bread, he gave it to Judas Iscariot, the son of Simon.

27. And after the morsel, Satan entered into him. And Jesus said to him, "What thou dost do quickly."

28. But none of those at the table understood why he said this to him.

29. For some thought that because Judas held the purse, Jesus had said to him "Buy the things we need for the feast"; or that he should give something to the poor.

30. When, therefore, he had received the morsel, he went out quickly. Now it was night.

From the Supper to the Agony in the Garden, Inclusive
(*Matt. 26: 30–46*)

30. And after reciting a hymn, they went out to Mount Olivet.

31. Then Jesus said to them, "You will all be scandalized this night because of me; for it is written, I will smite the shepherd, and the sheep of the flock will be scattered.

32. But after I have risen, I will go before you into Galilee."

33. But Peter answered and said to him, "Even though all shall be scandalized because of thee, I will never be scandalized."

34. Jesus said to him, "Amen I say to thee, this very night before a cock crows, thou wilt deny me three times."

35. Peter said to him, "Even if I should have to die with thee, I will not deny thee!" And all the disciples said the same thing.

36. Then Jesus came with them to a country place called Gethsemani, and he said to his disciples, "Sit down here, while I go over yonder and pray."

37. And he took with him Peter and the two sons of Zebedee, and he began to be saddened and exceedingly troubled.

38. Then he said to them, "My soul is sad even unto death. Wait here and watch with me."

39. And going forward a little, he fell prostrate and prayed saying, "Father, if it is possible, let this cup pass away from me; yet not as I will, but as thou willest."

40. Then he came to the disciples and found them sleeping. And he said to Peter, "Could you not, then, watch one hour with me?

41. Watch and pray, that you may not enter into temptation. The spirit indeed is willing, but the flesh is weak."

42. Again a second time he went away and prayed, saying, "My Father, if this cup cannot pass away unless I drink it, thy will be done."

43. And he came again and found them sleeping for their eyes were heavy.

44. And leaving them he went back again and prayed a third time, saying the same words over.

45. Then he came to his disciples and said to them, "Sleep on now, and take your rest! Behold the hour is at hand when the Son of man will be betrayed into the hands of sinners.

46. Rise, let us go. Behold, he who betrays me is at hand."

(Mark 14: 26–42)

26. And after reciting a hymn, they went out to the Mount of Olives.

27. And Jesus said to them, "You will all be scandalized this night; for it is written, I will smite the shepherd, and the sheep will be scattered.

28. But after I have risen, I will go before you into Galilee."

29. But Peter said to him, "Even though all shall be scandalized, yet not I."

30. Jesus said to him, "Amen I say to thee, today, this very night, before a cock crows twice, thou wilt deny me three times."

31. But he went on speaking more vehemently, "Even if I should have to die with thee, I will not deny thee!" And they all said the same thing.

32. And they came to a country place called Gethsemani, and he said to his disciples, "Sit down here, while I pray."

33. And he took with him Peter and James and John, and he began to feel dread and to be exceedingly troubled.

34. And he said to them, "My soul is sad even unto death. Wait here and watch."

35. And going forward a little, he fell on the ground, and began to pray that, if it were possible, the hour might pass from him;

36. And he said, "Abba, Father, all things are possible to thee. Remove this cup from me; yet not what I will, but what thou willest."

37. Then he came and found them sleeping. And he said to Peter, "Simon, dost thou sleep? Couldst thou not watch one hour?

38. Watch and pray, that you may not enter into temptation. The spirit indeed is willing, but the flesh is weak."

39. And again he went away and prayed, saying the same words over.

40. And he came again and found them sleeping, for their eyes were heavy. And they did not know what answer to make to him.

41. And he came the third time, and said to them, "Sleep on now, and take your rest! It is enough the hour has come. Behold, the Son of Man is betrayed into the hands of sinners.

42. Rise, let us go. Behold, he who will betray me is at hand."

From the Agony in the Garden
to the House of Annas, Inclusive
(*Matt.* 26: 47–56)

47. And while he was yet speaking, behold Judas one of the Twelve, came and with him a great crowd with swords and clubs, from the chief priests and elders of the people.

48. Now his betrayer had given them a sign, saying, "Whomever I kiss, that is he; lay hold of him."

49. And he went straight up to Jesus and said, "Hail Rabbi!" and kissed him.

50. And Jesus said to him, "Friend, for what purpose hast thou come?" Then they came forward and set hands on Jesus and took him.

51. And behold, one of those who were with Jesus reached out his hand, drew his sword, and struck the servant of the high priest, cutting off his ear.

52. Then Jesus said to him, "Put back thy sword into its place; for all those who take the sword will perish by the sword.

53. Or dost thou suppose that I cannot entreat my Father, and he will even now furnish me with more than twelve legions of angels?

54. How then are the Scriptures to be fulfilled, that thus it must take place?"

55. In that hour Jesus said to the crowds, "As against a robber you have come out, with swords and clubs, to seize me. I sat daily with you in the temple teaching, and you did not lay hands on me."

56. Now all this was done that the Scriptures of the prophets might be fulfilled. Then all the disciples left him and fled.

(*Luke* 22: 47–53)

47. And while he was yet speaking, behold a crowd came; and he who was called Judas, one of the Twelve, was going before them, and he drew near to Jesus to kiss him.
48. But Jesus said to him, "Judas, dost thou betray the Son of Man with a kiss?"
49. But when they who were about him saw what would follow, they said to him, "Lord, shall we strike with the sword?"
50. And one of them struck the servant of the high priest and cut off his right ear.
51. But Jesus answered and said, "Bear with them thus far." And he touched his ear and healed him.
52. But Jesus said to the chief priests and captains of the temple and elders, who had come against him, "As against a robber have you come out, with swords and clubs.
53. When I was daily with you in the temple, you did not stretch forth your hands against me. But this is your hour, and the power of darkness."

(*Mark* 14: 43–52)

43. And while he was yet speaking, Judas Iscariot, one of the Twelve, came and with him a great crowd with swords and clubs, from the chief priests and the Scribes and the elders.
44. Now his betrayer had given them a sign saying, "Whomever I kiss, that is he; lay hold of him, and lead him safely away."
45. And when he came, he went straight up to him, and said, "Rabbi!" and kissed him.
46. And they seized him and held him.
47. But one of the bystanders drew his sword, and struck the servant of the high priest, and cut off his ear.
48. And Jesus, addressing them, said, "As against a robber you have come out, with swords and clubs to seize me.

49. I was daily with you in the temple teaching, and you did not lay hands on me. But it is so that the Scriptures may be fulfilled."

50. Then all his disciples left him and fled.

51. And a certain young man was following him, having a linen cloth wrapped about his naked body, and they seized him.

52. But leaving the linen cloth behind, he fled away from them naked.

(John 18: 1–23)

1. After saying these things, Jesus went forth with his disciples beyond the torrent of Cedron, where there was a garden into which he and his disciples entered.

2. Now Judas, who betrayed him, also knew the place, since Jesus had often met there together with his disciples.

3. Judas then, taking the cohort, and attendants from the chief priests and Pharisees, came there with lanterns, and torches and weapons.

4. Jesus therefore knowing all that was to come upon him, went forth and said to them, "Whom do you seek?"

5. They answered him, "Jesus of Nazareth." Jesus said to them, "I am he." Now Judas who betrayed him, was also standing with them.

6. When, therefore, he said to them, "I am he," they drew back and fell to the ground.

7. So he asked them again, "Whom do you seek?" And they said, "Jesus of Nazareth."

8. Jesus answered, "I have told you that I am he. If, therefore, you seek me, let these go their way."

9. That the word which he said might be fulfilled, "Of those whom thou hast given me, I have not lost one."

10. Simon Peter therefore, having a sword, drew it and struck the servant of the high priest and cut off his right ear. Now the servant's name was Malchus.

11. Jesus therefore said to Peter, "Put up thy sword into the scabbard. Shall I not drink the cup that the Father has given me?"

12. The cohort therefore and the tribune and the attendants of the Jews seized Jesus and bound him.

13. And they brought him to Annas first, for he was the father-in-law of Caiphas, who was the high priest that year.

14. Now it was Caiphas who had given the counsel to the Jews that it was expedient that one man should die for the people.

15. But Simon Peter was following Jesus and so was another disciple. Now that disciple was known to the high priest, and he entered with Jesus into the courtyard of the high priest.

16. But Peter was standing outside at the gate. So the other disciple who was known to the high priest, went out and spoke to the portress, and brought Peter in.

17. The maid, who was portress, said therefore to Peter, "Art thou also one of this man's disciples?" He said, "I am not."

18. Now the servants and attendants were standing at a coal fire and warming themselves, for it was cold. And Peter also was with them, standing and warming himself.

19. The high priest therefore questioned Jesus concerning his disciples and concerning his teaching.

20. Jesus answered him, "I have spoken openly to the world; I have always taught in the synagogue and in the temple, where all the Jews gather, and in secret I have said nothing.

21. Why dost thou question me? Question those who have heard what I spoke to them; behold, these know what I have said."

22. Now when he had said these things, one of the attendants who was standing by struck Jesus a blow, saying, "Is that the way thou dost answer the high priest?"

23. Jesus answered him. "If I have spoken ill, bear witness to the evil; but if well, why dost thou strike me?"

FROM THE HOUSE OF ANNAS
TO THE HOUSE OF CAIPHAS, INCLUSIVE
(*Matt.* 26: 57–75)

57. Now those who had taken Jesus led him away to Caiphas the high priest, where the Scribes and the elders had gathered together.

58. But Peter was following him at a distance, even to the courtyard of the high priest, and he went in and sat with the attendants to see the end.

59. Now the chief priests and all the Sanhedrin were seeking false witness against Jesus, that they might put him to death,

60. but they found none, though many false witnesses came forward. But last of all two false witnesses came forward,

61. and said, "This man said, 'I am able to destroy the temple of God, and to rebuild it after three days.'"

62. Then the high priest, standing up, said to him, "Dost thou make no answer to the things that these men prefer against thee?"

63. But Jesus kept silence. And the high priest said to him, "I adjure thee by the living God that thou tell us whether thou art the Christ, the Son of God."

64. Jesus said to him, "Thou hast said it. Nevertheless, I say to you, hereafter you shall see the Son of Man sitting at the right hand of the Power and coming upon the clouds of heaven."

65. Then the high priest tore his garments, saying, "He has blasphemed; what further need have we of witnesses? Behold now you have heard the blasphemy.

66. What do you think?" and they answered and said, "He is liable to death."

67. Then they spat in his face and buffeted him; while others struck his face with the palms of their hands,

68. saying, "Prophesy to us, O Christ! who is it that struck thee?"

69. Now Peter was sitting outside in the courtyard and a maidservant came up to him and said, "Thou also wast with Jesus the Galilean."

70. But he denied it before them all saying, "I do not know what thou art saying."

71. And when he had gone out to the gateway, another maid saw him, and said to those who were there, "This man also was with Jesus of Nazareth."

72. And again he denied it with an oath, "I do not know the man!"

73. And after a little while the bystanders came up and said to Peter, "Surely thou also art one of them, for even thy speech betrays thee."

74. Then he began to curse and to swear that he did not know the man. And at that moment a cock crowed.

75. And Peter remembered the word that Jesus had said, "Before a cock crows, thou wilt deny me three times." And he went out and wept bitterly.

(Mark 14: 53–72)

53. And they led Jesus away to the high priest; and all the priests and the Scribes and the elders gathered together.

54. But Peter followed him at a distance, even to the court-yard of the high priest, and was sitting with the attendants at the fire and warming himself.

55. Now the chief priests and all the Sanhedrin were seeking witness against Jesus, that they might put him to death, but they found none.

56. For while many bore false witness against him, their evidence did not agree.

57. And some stood up and bore false witness against him, saying,

58. "We ourselves have heard him say, 'I will destroy this temple built by hands, and after three days I will build an-other, not built by hands.'"

59. And even then their evidence did not agree.

60. Then the high priest standing up in their midst, asked Jesus, saying, "Dost thou make no answer to the things that these men prefer against thee?"

61. But he kept silence, and made no answer. Again the high priest began to ask him, and said to him, "Art thou the Christ, the Son of the Blessed One?"

62. And Jesus said to him, "I am. And you shall see the Son of Man sitting at the right hand of the Power and com-ing with the clouds of heaven."

63. But the high priest tore his garments and said, "What further need have we of witnesses?

64. You have heard the blasphemy. What do you think?" And they all condemned him as liable to death.

65. And some began to spit on him, and to blindfold him, and to buffet him, and to say to him, "Prophesy." And the attendants struck him with blows of their hands.

66. And while Peter was below in the courtyard, there came one of the maidservants of the high priest;

67. and seeing Peter warming himself she looked closely at him and said, "Thou also wast with Jesus of Nazareth."

68. But he denied it, saying, "I neither know nor understand what thou art saying." And he went outside into the vestibule; and the cock crowed.

69. And the maidservant, seeing him again, began to say to the bystanders, "This is one of them."

70. But again he denied it. And after a little while the bystanders again said to Peter, "Surely thou art one of them, for thou art also a Galilean."

71. But he began to curse and to swear; "I do not know this man you are talking about."

72. And at that moment a cock crowed a second time. And Peter remembered the word that Jesus had said to him, "Before a cock crows twice, thou wilt deny me three times." And he began to weep.

(*Luke 22: 54–65*)

54. Now having seized him, they led him away to the high priest's house; but Peter was following at a distance.

55. And when they had kindled a fire in the middle of the courtyard, and were seated together, Peter was in their midst.

56. But a certain maidservant saw him sitting at the blaze, and after gazing upon him she said, "This man too was with him."

57. But he denied him, saying, "Woman, I do not know him."

58. And after a little while someone else saw him and said, "Thou, too, art one of them." But Peter said, "Man, I am not."

59. And about an hour later another insisted, saying, "Surely this man, too, was with him, for he also is a Galilean."

60. But Peter said, "Man, I do not know what thou sayest."

And at that moment, while he was yet speaking, a cock crowed.

61. And the Lord turned and looked upon Peter. And Peter remembered the word of the Lord, how he said, "Before a cock crows, thou wilt deny me three times."

62. And Peter went out and wept bitterly.

63. And the men who had him in custody began to mock him and beat him.

64. And they blindfolded him, and kept striking his face and asking him, saying, "Prophesy, who is it that struck thee?"

65. And many other things they kept saying against him, reviling him.

FROM THE HOUSE OF CAIPHAS
TO THE HOUSE OF PILATE, INCLUSIVE
(*Matt.* 27: 1–26)

1. Now when morning came all the chief priests and the elders of the people took counsel together against Jesus in order to put him to death.

2. And they bound him and led him away, and delivered him to Pontius Pilate the procurator.

3. Then Judas, who betrayed him, when he saw that he was condemned, repented and brought back the thirty pieces of silver to the chief priests and the elders,

4. saying, "I have sinned in betraying innocent blood." But they said, "What is that to us? See to it thyself."

5. And he flung the pieces of silver into the temple, and withdrew; and went away and hanged himself with a halter.

6. And the chief priests took the pieces of silver, and said, "It is not lawful to put them into the treasury, seeing that it is the price of blood."

7. And after they had consulted together, they bought with them the potter's field, as a burial place for strangers.

8. For this reason that field has been called even to this day, Haceldama, that is, the Field of Blood.

9. Then what was spoken through Jeremias the prophet was fulfilled, *And they took the thirty pieces of silver, the price*

of him who was priced upon whom the children of Israel set a price;

10. *and they gave them for the potter's field, as the Lord directed me.*

11. Now Jesus stood before the procurator, and the procurator asked him, saying, "Art thou the king of the Jews?" Jesus said to him, "Thou sayest it."

12. And when he was accused by the chief priests and the elders, he made no answer.

13. Then Pilate said to him, "Dost thou not hear how many things they prefer against thee?"

14. But he did not answer him a single word, so that the procurator wondered exceedingly.

15. Now at festival time the procurator used to release to the crowd a prisoner, whomever they would.

16. Now he had at that time a notorious prisoner called Barabbas.

17. Therefore, when they had gathered together, Pilate said, "Whom do you wish that I release to you? Barabbas, or Jesus who is called Christ?"

18. For he knew that they had delivered him up out of envy.

19. Now, as he was sitting on the judgment-seat, his wife sent to him, saying, "Have nothing to do with that just man, for I have suffered many things in a dream today because of him."

20. But the chief priests and the elders persuaded the crowds to ask for Barabbas and to destroy Jesus.

21. But the procurator addressed them and said to them, "Which of the two do you wish that I release to you?" And they said, "Barabbas."

22. Pilate said to them, "What then am I to do with Jesus who is called Christ?"

23. They all said, "Let him be crucified!" The procurator said to them, "Why, what evil has he done?" But they kept crying out the more, saying, "Let him be crucified!"

24. Now Pilate, seeing that he was doing no good, but rather that a riot was breaking out, took water and washed his hands in sight of the crowd, saying, "I am innocent of the blood of this just man; see to it yourselves."

25. And all the people answered and said, "His blood be on us and on our children."

26. Then he released to them Barabbas; but Jesus he scourged and delivered to them to be crucified.

(Luke 23: 1–5)

1. And the whole assemblage rose, and took him before Pilate.

2. And they began to accuse him saying, "We have found this man perverting our nation, and forbidding the payment of taxes to Caesar, and saying that he is Christ a king."

3. So Pilate asked him saying, "Art thou the king of the Jews?" And he answered him and said, "Thou sayest it."

4. And Pilate said to the chief priests and to the crowds, "I find no guilt in this man."

5. But they persisted, saying, "He is stirring up the people teaching throughout all Judea, and beginning from Galilee even to this place."

(Mark 15: 1–15)

1. And as soon as it was morning, the chief priests held a consultation with the elders, the Scribes and the whole Sanhedrin. And they bound Jesus and led him away, and delivered him to Pilate.

2. And Pilate asked him, "Art thou the king of the Jews?" And he answered him and said, "Thou sayest it."

3. And the chief priests accused him of many things.

4. And Pilate again asked him, saying "Hast thou no answer to make? Behold how many things they accuse thee of."

5. But Jesus made no further answer, so that Pilate wondered.

6. Now at festival time he used to release to them one of the prisoners, whomever they had petitioned for.

7. Now there was a man called Barabbas imprisoned with some rioters, one who in the riot had committed murder.

8. And the crowd came up, and began to ask that he do for them as he was wont.

9. But Pilate addressed them, saying, "Do you wish that I release to you the king of the Jews?"

10. For he knew that the chief priests had delivered him up out of envy.

11. But the chief priests stirred up the crowd to have him release Barabbas for them instead.

12. But Pilate again spoke and said to them, "What then do you want me to do to the king of the Jews?"

13. But they cried out again, "Crucify him!"

14. But Pilate said to them, "Why, what evil has he done?" But they kept crying out the more, "Crucify him!"

15. So Pilate, wishing to satisfy the crowd, released to them Barabbas; but Jesus he scourged and delivered to be crucified.

FROM THE HOUSE OF PILATE
TO THE HOUSE OF HEROD
(Luke 23: 6–10)

6. But Pilate hearing Galilee, asked whether the man was a Galilean.

7. And learning that he belonged to Herod's jurisdiction, he sent him back to Herod, who likewise was in Jerusalem in those days.

8. Now when Herod saw Jesus he was exceedingly glad; for he had been a long time desirous to see him, because he had heard so much about him, and he was hoping to see some miracle done by him.

9. Now he put many questions to him but he made him no answer.

10. Now the chief priests and Scribes were standing by, vehemently accusing him.

FROM THE HOUSE OF HEROD
TO THAT OF PILATE
(Matt. 27: 24–30)

24. Now Pilate seeing that he was doing no good, but rather that a riot was breaking out, took water and washed his hands in sight of the crowd, saying, "I am innocent of the blood of this just man; see to it yourselves."

25. And all the people answered and said, "His blood be on us and on our children."

26. Then he released to them Barabbas; but Jesus he scourged and delivered to them to be crucified.

27. Then the soldiers of the procurator took Jesus into the praetorium, and gathered together about him the whole cohort.

28. And they stripped him and put on him a scarlet cloak;

29. and plaiting a crown of thorns, they put it upon his head, and a reed into his right hand; and bending the knee before him they mocked him, saying, "Hail, King of the Jews!"

30. And they spat on him, and took the reed and kept striking him on the head.

(Luke 23: 12–23)

12. And Herod and Pilate became friends that very day; whereas previously they had been at enmity with each other.

13. And Pilate called together the chief priests and the rulers and the people,

14. and said to them, "You have brought before me this man, as one who perverts the people; and behold, I upon examining him in your presence have found no guilt in this man as touching those things of which you accuse him.

15. Neither has Herod; for I sent you back to him, and behold, nothing deserving of death has been committed by him.

16. I will therefore chastise him and release him."

17. Now at the festival time it was necessary for him to release to them one prisoner.

18. But the whole mob cried out together saying, "Away with this man, and release to us Barabbas!"—

19. one who had been thrown into prison for a certain riot that had occurred in the city, and for murder.

20. But Pilate spoke to them again, wishing to release Jesus.

21. But they kept shouting, saying, "Crucify him! Crucify him!"

22. And he said to them a third time, "Why, what evil has this man done? I find no crime deserving of death in him. I will therefore chastise him and release him."

23. But they persisted with loud cries, demanding that he should be crucified; and their cries prevailed.

(Mark 15: 15–19)

15. So Pilate, wishing to satisfy the crowd, released to them Barabbas; but Jesus he scourged and delivered to be crucified.
16. Now the soldiers led him away into the courtyard of the praetorium, and they called together the whole cohort.
17. And they clothed him in purple, and plaiting a crown of thorns, they put it upon him,
18. and began to greet him, "Hail, King of the Jews!"
19. And they kept striking him on the head with a reed, and spitting upon him; and bending their knees, they did homage to him.

(John 19: 1–11)

1. Pilate, then, took Jesus and had him scourged.
2. And the soldiers, plaiting a crown of thorns, put it upon his head, and arrayed him in a purple cloak.
3. And they kept coming to him and saying, "Hail, King of the Jews!" and striking him.
4. Pilate therefore again went outside and said to them, "Behold, I bring him out to you, that you may know that I find no guilt in him."
5. Jesus therefore came forth, wearing the crown of thorns and the purple cloak. And he said to them, "Behold, the man!"
6. When, therefore, the chief priests and the attendants saw him, they cried out, saying, "Crucify him! Crucify him!" Pilate said to them, "Take him yourselves and crucify him, for I find no guilt in him."
7. The Jews answered him, "We have a Law, and according to that Law he must die, because he has made himself Son of God."
8. Now when Pilate heard this statement, he feared the more.
9. And he again went back into the praetorium, and said to

Jesus, "Where art thou from?" But Jesus gave him no answer.

10. Pilate therefore said to him, "Dost thou not speak to me? Dost thou not know that I have power to crucify thee, and that I have power to release thee?"

11. Jesus answered, "Thou wouldst have no power at all over me were it not given thee from above. Therefore, he who betrayed me to thee has the greater sin."

From the House of Pilate to the Cross, Inclusive
(John 19: 12–24)

12. And from then on Pilate was looking for a way to release him. But the Jews cried out, saying, "If thou release this man, thou art no friend of Caesar; for everyone who makes himself king sets himself against Caesar."

13. Pilate therefore, when he heard these words, brought Jesus outside, and sat down on the judgment-seat, at a place called Lithostrotos, but in Hebrew, Gabbatha.

14. Now it was the Preparation Day for the Passover about the sixth hour. And he said to the Jews, "Behold, your king!"

15. But they cried out, "Away with him! Away with him! Crucify him!" Pilate said to them, "Shall I crucify your king?" The chief priests answered, "We have no king but Caesar."

16. Then he handed him over to them to be crucified. And so they took Jesus and led him away.

17. And bearing the cross for himself, he went forth to the place called the Skull, in Hebrew, Golgotha,

18. where they crucified him, and with him two others, one on each side and Jesus in the center.

19. And Pilate also wrote an inscription and had it put on the cross. And there was written, JESUS OF NAZARETH, THE KING OF THE JEWS.

20. Many of the Jews therefore read this inscription, because the place where Jesus was crucified was near the city; and it was written in Hebrew, in Greek and in Latin.

21. The chief priests of the Jews said therefore to Pilate, "Do

not write, 'The King of the Jews,' but, 'He said, I am the King of the Jews.'"

22. Pilate answered, "What I have written, I have written."

23. The soldiers therefore, when they had crucified him, took his garments and made of them four parts, to each soldier a part, and also the tunic. Now the tunic was without seam, woven in one piece from the top.

24. They therefore said to one another, "Let us not tear it, but let us cast lots for it, to see whose it shall be." That the scriptures might be fulfilled which says, *They divided my garments among them; and for my vesture they cast lots.* These things therefore the soldiers did.

Jesus upon the Cross
(John 19: 23–37)

23. The soldiers therefore, when they had crucified him, took his garments and made of them four parts, to each soldier a part, and also the tunic. Now the tunic was without seam, woven in one piece from the top.

24. They therefore said to one another, "Let us not tear it, but let us cast lots for it, to see whose it shall be." That the scriptures might be fulfilled which says, *They divided my garments among them; and for my vesture they cast lots.* These things therefore the soldiers did.

25. Now there were standing by the cross of Jesus his mother and his mother's sister, Mary of Cleophas, and Mary Magdalene.

26. When Jesus therefore, saw his mother and the disciple standing by, whom he loved, he said to his mother, "Woman, behold thy son."

27. Then he said to the disciple, "Behold thy mother." And from that hour the disciple took her into his home.

28. After this Jesus, knowing that all things were now accomplished, that the Scripture might be fulfilled, said, "I thirst."

29. Now there was standing there a vessel full of common wine; and having put a sponge soaked with the wine on a stalk of hyssop, they put it to his mouth.

30. Therefore, when Jesus had taken the wine, he said, "It is consummated!" And bowing his head he gave up his spirit.
31. The Jews therefore, since it was the Preparation Day, in order that the bodies might not remain upon the cross on the Sabbath (for that Sabbath was a solemn day), besought Pilate that their legs might be broken, and that they might be taken away.
32. The soldiers therefore came and broke the legs of the first, and of the other, who had been crucified with him.
33. But when they came to Jesus, and saw that he was already dead, they did not break his legs;
34. but one of the soldiers opened his side with a lance, and immediately there came out blood and water.
35. And he who saw it has borne witness, and his witness is true; and he knows that he tells the truth, that you also may believe.
36. For these things came to pass that the Scripture might be fulfilled, Not a bone of him shall you break.
37. And again another Scripture says, They shall look upon him whom they have pierced.

(Matt. 27: 35–39)

35. And after they had crucified him, they divided his garments, casting lots, [to fulfill what was spoken through the prophet, *They divided my garments among them, and upon my vesture they cast lots.*]
36. And sitting down they kept watch over him.
37. And they put above his head the charge against him, written, THIS IS JESUS, THE KING OF THE JEWS.
38. Then two robbers were crucified with him, one on his right hand and one on his left.
39. Now the passers-by were jeering at him shaking their heads,

(Mark 15: 24–38)

24. Then they crucified him, and divided his garments, casting lots for them to see what each should take.

25. Now it was the third hour and they crucified him.

26. And the inscription bearing the charge against him was, THE KING OF THE JEWS.

27. And they crucified two robbers with him, one on his right hand and one on his left.

28. And the Scripture was fulfilled, which says, *And he was reckoned among the wicked.*

29. And the passers-by were jeering at him, shaking their heads, and saying, "Aha, thou who destroyed the temple, and in three days buildest it up again;

30. come down from the cross, and save thyself!"

31. In like manner, the chief priests with the Scribes said in mockery to one another, "He saved others, himself he cannot save!

32. Let the Christ, the King of Israel, come down now from the cross, that we may see and believe." And they who were crucified with him reproached him.

33. And when the sixth hour came, there was darkness over the whole land until the ninth hour.

34. And at the ninth hour Jesus cried out with a loud voice, saying, "Eloi, Eloi, lama sabacthani?" which, translated, is, "My God, my God, why hast thou forsaken me?"

35. And some of the bystanders on hearing this said, "Behold, he is calling Elias."

36. But someone ran, soaked a sponge in common wine, and put it on a reed and offered it to him to drink, saying, "Wait, let us see whether Elias is coming to take him down."

37. But Jesus cried out with a loud voice, and expired.

38. And the curtain of the temple was torn in two from top to bottom.

(Luke 23: 34–46)

34. And Jesus said, "Father, forgive them, for they do not know what they are doing." Now in dividing his garments, they cast lots.

35. And the people stood looking on; and the rulers with them kept sneering at him, saying, "He saved others, let him save himself, if he is the Christ, the chosen one of God."

36. And the soldiers also mocked him, coming to him and offering him common wine,

37. and saying, "If thou art the King of the Jews, save thyself!"

38. And there was also an inscription written over him in Greek and Latin and Hebrew letters, THIS IS THE KING OF THE JEWS.

39. Now one of those robbers who were hanged was abusing him, saying, "If thou art the Christ, save thyself and us!"

40. But the other in answer rebuked him and said, "Dost not even thou fear God, seeing that thou art under the same sentence?

41. And we indeed justly, for we are receiving what our deeds deserved; but this man has done nothing wrong."

42. And he said to Jesus, "Lord, remember me when thou comest into thy kingdom."

43. And Jesus said to him, "Amen I say to thee, this day thou shalt be with me in paradise."

44. It was now about the sixth hour, and there was darkness over the whole land until the ninth hour.

45. And the sun was darkened, and the curtain of the temple was torn in the middle.

46. And Jesus cried out with a loud voice and said, "Father, into thy hands I commend my spirit." And having said this, he expired.

FROM THE CROSS TO THE SEPULCHER, INCLUSIVE
(John 19: 38–42)

38. Now after these things Joseph of Arimathea, because he was a disciple of Jesus (although for fear of the Jews a secret one), besought Pilate that he might take away the body of Jesus. And Pilate gave permission. He came, therefore, and took away the body of Jesus.

39. And there also came Nicodemus (who at first had come to Jesus by night), bringing a mixture of myrrh and aloes, in weight about a hundred pounds.

40. They therefore took the body of Jesus and wrapped it in linen cloths with the spices, after the Jewish manner of preparing for burial.

41. Now in the place where he was crucified there was a garden, and in the garden a new tomb in which no one had yet been laid.

42. There, accordingly, because of the Preparation Day of the Jews, for the tomb was close at hand, they laid Jesus.

THE SECOND APPARITION
(*Mark 16: 1–11*)

1. And when the Sabbath was past, Mary Magdalene, Mary the mother of Jesus, and Salome, bought spices, that they might go and anoint him.

2. And very early on the first day of the week, they came to the tomb, when the sun had just risen.

3. And they were saying to one another, "Who will roll the stone back from the entrance of the tomb for us?"

4. And looking up they saw that the stone had been rolled back, for it was very large.

5. But on entering the tomb, they saw a young man sitting at the right side, clothed in a white robe, and they were amazed.

6. He said to them, "Do not be terrified. You are looking for Jesus of Nazareth, who was crucified. He has risen, he is not here. Behold the place where they laid him.

7. But go tell his disciples and Peter that he goes before you into Galilee: there you shall see him, as he told you."

8. And they departed and fled from the tomb, for trembling and fear had seized them; and they said nothing to anyone, for they were afraid.

9. Now when he had risen from the dead early on the first day of the week, he appeared first to Mary Magdalene, out of whom he had cast seven devils.

10. She went and brought word to those who had been with him, as they were mourning and weeping.

11. And they, hearing that he was alive and had been seen by her, did not believe it.

THE THIRD APPARITION
(*Matt. 28: 8–10*)

8. And they departed quickly from the tomb in fear and great joy, and ran to tell his disciples.

9. And behold Jesus met them, saying, "Hail!" And they came up and embraced his feet and worshipped him.

10. Then Jesus said to them, "Do not be afraid; go, take word to my brethren that they are to set out for Galilee; there they shall see me."

THE FOURTH APPARITION
(*Luke 24: 10–12*)

10. Now, it was Mary Magdalene and Joanna and Mary, the mother of James, and the other women who were with them, who were telling these things to the apostles.

11. But this tale seemed to them to be nonsense, and they did not believe the women.

12. But Peter arose and ran to the tomb; and stooping down, he saw the linen cloths laid there; and he went away wondering to himself at what had come to pass.

(*Luke 24: 33–34*)

33. And rising up that very hour, they returned to Jerusalem, where they found the Eleven gathered together and those who were with them,

34. saying, "The Lord has risen indeed, and has appeared to Simon."

THE FIFTH APPARITION
(*Luke 24: 13–35*)

13. And behold, two of them were going that very day to a village named Emmaus, which is sixty stadia from Jerusalem.

14. And they were talking to each other about all these things that had happened.

15. And it came to pass, while they were conversing and arguing together, that Jesus himself also drew near and went along with them;

16. but their eyes were held, that they should not recognize him.

17. And he said to them, "What words are these that you are exchanging as you walk and are sad?"

18. But one of them, named Cleophas, answered and said to him, "Art thou the only stranger in Jerusalem who does not know the things that have happened there in these days?"
19. And he said to them, "What things?" And they said to him, "Concerning Jesus of Nazareth, who was a prophet, mighty in work and word before God and all the people;
20. and how our chief priests and rulers delivered him up to be sentenced to death, and crucified him.
21. But we were hoping that it was he who should redeem Israel. Yes, and besides all this, today is the third day since these things came to pass.
22. And moreover, certain women of our company, who were at the tomb before it was light, astounded us,
23. and not finding his body, they came, saying that they had also seen a vision of angels, who said that he is alive.
24. So some of our company went to the tomb, and found it even as the women had said, but him they did not see."
25. But he said to them, "O foolish ones and slow of heart to believe in all that the prophets have spoken!
26. Did not the Christ have to suffer these things before entering into his glory?"
27. And beginning then with Moses and with all the Prophets, he interpreted to them in all the Scriptures the things referring to himself.
28. And they drew near to the village to which they were going, and he acted as though he were going on.
29. And they urged him, saying, "Stay with us, for it is getting towards evening and the day is now far spent." And he went in with them.
30. And it came to pass when he reclined at table with them, that he took the bread and blessed and broke and began handing it to them.
31. And their eyes were opened, and they recognized him; and he vanished from their sight.
32. And they said to each other, "Was not our heart burning within us while he was speaking on the road and explaining to us the Scriptures?"

33. And rising up that very hour, they returned to Jerusalem, where they found the Eleven gathered together and those who were with them,

34. saying, "The Lord has risen indeed, and has appeared to Simon."

35. And they themselves began to relate what had happened on the journey, and how they recognized him in the breaking of the bread.

THE SIXTH APPARITION
(John 20: 19–23)

19. When it was late that same day, the first of the week, though the doors where the disciples gathered had been closed for fear of the Jews, Jesus came and stood in the midst and said to them, "Peace be to you!"

20. And when he had said this, he showed them his hands and his side. The disciples therefore rejoiced at the sight of the Lord.

21. He therefore said to them again, "Peace be to you! As the Father has sent me, I also send you."

22. When he had said this, he breathed upon them, and said to them, "Receive the Holy Spirit;

23. whose sins you shall forgive, they are forgiven them; and whose sins you shall retain, they are retained."

THE SEVENTH APPARITION
(John 20: 24–29)

24. Now Thomas, one of the Twelve called the Twin, was not with them when Jesus came.

25. The other disciples therefore said to him, "We have seen the Lord." But he said to them, "Unless I see in his hands the print of the nails, and put my finger into the place of the nails, and put my hand into his side, I will not believe."

26. And after eight days his disciples were again inside, and Thomas with them, Jesus came, the doors being closed, and stood in their midst, and said, "Peace be to you!"

27. Then he said to Thomas, "Bring here thy finger, and see my hands; and bring here thy hand, and put it into my side; and be not unbelieving but believing."

28. Thomas answered and said to him, "My Lord and my God!"

29. Jesus said to him, "Because thou hast seen me, thou hast believed. Blessed are they who have not seen, and yet have believed."

THE EIGHTH APPARITION
(John 21: 1–17)

1. After these things, Jesus manifested himself again at the sea of Tiberias. Now he manifested himself in this way.

2. There were together Simon Peter and Thomas, called the Twin, and Nathanael, from Cana in Galilee, and the sons of Zebedee, and two others of his disciples.

3. Simon Peter said to them, "I am going fishing." They said to him, "We also are going with thee." And they went out and got into the boat. And that night they caught nothing.

4. But when the day was breaking, Jesus stood on the beach; yet the disciples did not know that it was Jesus.

5. Then Jesus said to them, "Young men, have you any fish?" They answered him, "No."

6. He said to them, "Cast the net to the right of the boat and you will find them." They cast therefore, and now they were unable to draw it up for the great number of fishes.

7. The disciple whom Jesus loved said therefore to Peter, "It is the Lord." Simon Peter therefore, hearing that it was the Lord, girt his tunic about him, for he was stripped, and threw himself into the sea.

8. But the other disciples came with the boat (for they were not far from land, only about two hundred cubits off), dragging the net full of fishes.

9. When, therefore, they had landed, they saw a fire ready, and a fish laid upon it, and bread.

10. Jesus said to them, "Bring here some of the fishes that you caught just now."

11. Simon Peter went aboard and hauled the net onto the land full of large fishes, one hundred and fifty-three in number. And though there were so many, the net was not torn.

12. Jesus said to them, "Come and breakfast." And none of those reclining dared ask him, "Who art thou?" knowing that it was the Lord.

13. And Jesus came and took the bread, and gave it to them, and likewise the fish.

14. This is now the third time that Jesus appeared to the disciples after he had risen from the dead.

15. When, therefore, they had breakfasted, Jesus said to Simon Peter, "Simon, son of John, dost thou love me more than these do?" He said to him, "Yes, Lord, thou knowest that I love thee." He said to him, "Feed my lambs."

16. He said to him a second time, "Simon, son of John, dost thou love me?" He said to him, "Yes, Lord, thou knowest that I love thee." He said to him, "Feed my lambs."

17. A third time he said to him, "Simon, son of John, dost thou love me?" Peter was grieved because he said to him for the third time, "Dost thou love me?" And he said to him, "Lord, thou knowest all things, thou knowest that I love thee." He said to him, "Feed my sheep."

THE NINTH APPARITION
(*Matt.* 28: 16–20)

16. But the eleven disciples went into Galilee, to the mountain where Jesus had directed them to go.

17. And when they saw him they worshipped him; but some doubted.

18. And Jesus drew near and spoke to them, saying, "All power in heaven and on earth has been given to me.

19. Go, therefore, and make disciples of all nations, baptizing them in the name of the Father, and of the Son, and of the Holy Spirit.

20. Teaching them to observe all that I have commanded you; and behold, I am with you all days, even unto the consummation of the world."

THE TENTH APPARITION
(*I Cor.* 15: 6)

6. Then he was seen by more than five hundred brethren at one time, many of whom are with us still, but some have fallen asleep.

THE ELEVENTH APPARITION
(*I Cor.* 15: 7)

7. After that he was seen by James, then by all the apostles.

THE THIRTEENTH APPARITION
(*I Cor.* 15: 8)

8. And last of all, as by one born out of due time, he was seen also by me.

THE ASCENSION OF CHRIST OUR LORD
(*Acts* 1: 1–11)

1. In the former book, O Theophilus, I spoke of all that Jesus did and taught from the beginning.
2. until the day on which he was taken through the Holy Spirit to the apostle whom he had chosen.
3. To them also he showed himself alive after his passion by many proofs, during forty days appearing to them and speaking of the kingdom of God.
4. And while eating with them, he charged them not to depart from Jerusalem, but to wait for the promise of the Father, "of which you have heard," said he, "by my mouth;
5. for John indeed baptized with water, but you shall be baptized with the Holy Spirit not many days hence."
6. They therefore who had come together began to ask him, saying, "Lord, wilt thou at this time restore the kingdom to Israel?"
7. But he said to them, "It is not for you to know the times or dates which the Father has fixed by his own authority;
8. but you shall receive power when the Holy Spirit comes

upon you, and you shall be witnesses for me in Jerusalem and in all Judea and Samaria and even to the very ends of the earth."

9. And when he had said this, he was lifted up before their eyes, and a cloud took him out of their sight.

10. And while they were gazing up to heaven as he went, behold, two men stood by them in white garments,

11. and said to them, "Men of Galilee, why do you stand looking up to heaven? This Jesus who has been taken up from you into heaven, shall come in the same way as you have seen him going up to heaven."

IMAGE BOOKS
OF CONTEMPLATION

AVAILABLE AT YOUR LOCAL BOOKSTORE OR YOU MAY USE THIS COUPON TO ORDER DIRECT.

ISBN	TITLE AND AUTHOR	PRICE	QTY.	TOTAL
41147-2	**Concise History of the Catholic Church** by Thomas Bokenkotter *A valuable sourcebook; a must for every teacher and library.*	U.S. **$12.95** / CAN. **$17.95**	x ___ =	_____
41961-9	**Maimonides** by Abraham J. Heschel *The life and times of the great medieval Jewish thinker.*	U.S. **$10.00** / CAN. **$13.00**	x ___ =	_____
42110-9	**Religion and the Rise of Western Culture** by Christopher Dawson *The classic study of medieval civilization.*	U.S. **$12.50** / CAN. **$17.50**	x ___ =	_____
42109-5	**Saint Joan of Arc** by V. Sackville-West *A biography with a beauty and reverence from which the last grain of sentimentality has been refined away. The result is pure gold.*	U.S. **$13.95** / CAN. **$17.95**	x ___ =	_____
42278-4	**Luther** by Heiko A. Oberman *This is the biography of Luther for our time by the world's foremost authority on Luther.*	U.S. **$15.00** / CAN. **$19.00**	x ___ =	_____

SHIPPING AND HANDLING:
Parcel Post . . . . . (add **$2.50 per order;** allow **4–6 weeks** for delivery) _____
UPS . . . . (add **$4.50 per order;** allow **2–3 weeks** for delivery) _____

TOTAL: _____

Please send me the titles I have indicated above. I am enclosing $_____.
Send check or money order (no CODs or cash, please) payable to Doubleday
Consumer Services. Prices and availability are subject to change without notice.

Name: _____

Address: _____ Apt. #: _____

City: _____ State: _____ Zip: _____

Send completed coupon and payment to:
Doubleday Consumer Services, Dept. IM**15**
2451 South Wolf Road
Des Plaines, IL 60018

IMAGE

IM15 - 10/95

BOOKS OF
SPIRITUAL
NOURISHMENT